Luck o' the Draw

Irish Gunfighters in the West

by
Karen Wilkes

Publisher: Karen E. Wilkes

karenwilkesnv@gmail.com

Cover and design by Darryl Martin

Also By Karen Wilkes

—Blue Sky and a Buick

—Bishop on Horseback

—Trampin' In, Pard

—Boot Hill Stories

For My Husband

Darryl Martin

Introduction

I was raised in a time warp, in a remote area of a very sparsely populated state. Pioche, Nevada, an 1870's silver ore boomtown, was my home. Located in southeastern Nevada within the area known as the Great Basin, Pioche is cradled between two of the Highland Range mountains at an elevation of about 6,000 feet. This was one of the last Nevada mountain ranges to be prospected for silver and gold after the "Big Bonanza" in Virginia City.

The pinion and juniper tree covered hills are steep, sporting a real western town which meanders haphazardly down the lower slopes descending to a sleepy sage-covered valley below. The weather is delightful in the summer and bitter cold in the winter. In short, if a winter snowfall sticks to the ground, you need a four-wheel drive vehicle to get groceries and check the mail.

In 1928, my grandfather, a hard-rock miner (sometimes mine superintendent in his best days) drove west with his wife and two children from Colorado looking for new, promising opportunities. They had done this numerous times during the past 10 years of their marriage. The family stopped in Las Vegas, but after a two-week look-around, my grandfather said, "This town will never amount to much; let's drive on up to Pioche and see what's going on." While slowly climbing the final grade on the high road into town, their trusty Model A, which had seen almost as many miles as mining towns, threw a rod. Grandpa nursed the old girl to the top of the grade and then coasted down Main Street, slowly taking the first available parking spot on the east side of the street in front of the barber shop.

By then, Grandpa was in his late 40's and had suffered a major hearing loss from too many years of exposure to loud mining equipment and underground blasting. No longer able to get underground mining jobs, he parked his family along with the Model A in Pioche while he explored other nearby mining camps for employment. Several years later he died of a heart attack, leaving my grandmother in a two-room miner's cabin nestled near the lower reaches of the famous Treasure Hill, where by 1921, twenty-five million dollars of rich silver ore had been extracted.

Grandma had two beds, a couple of pots and pans, a can of lard on the back of the stove, a fistful of flour, and two kids. This was life for many Americans in 1930.

Amazingly enough, Grandma and both kids thrived in Pioche. There was a lot of community spirit and sharing of goods. At some point Grandma even saved enough money to buy a used upright grand piano, which she managed to fit into her miner's cabin. Her theory was that if her children could learn to play the piano, they would be cultured. In time I inherited the piano and managed to move it to and from several different States — each move requiring at least six strong men — and I'm still not sure about the 'cultured' aspect. However, with the support of the town and a very focused mother, the kids did well. My dad, a World War II war hero, became a lawyer, and my aunt a high school English teacher.

I grew up in a house originally built by Combined Metals Co. for management families, which later after they ceased their mining operation, became available for sale to the public. Yes, the treasure had been depleted, and the Corporation had closed up shop. The living room windows on the east side of the house overlooked a high desert landscape, an abandoned mining building left over from someone's dream, and the legendary "Boot Hill" cemetery.

Boot Hill was the original 1860's graveyard where it is rumored that 72 men died with their boots on (meaning they died a violent death – a stigma at that time) before one man died of natural causes. This historic graveyard was about two blocks from my house, just one part of the decaying past that became my playground. On any given weekend, a trip through Boot Hill might be part of a short walk through the desert looking for cool stuff that we could drag home and add to our playhouse — like purple bottles, tin sardine and tobacco cans, rusty plates, cups, and maybe an old boot or lace up shoe. There were 269 people buried in Boot Hill between the years 1868 and 1875, and no one knows exactly where each body was laid to rest. However, the County does have records of each death, and the bodies are, in fact, somewhere in that cemetery.

The infamous gunfighter, Morgan Courtney, was #186 on the roster of recorded deaths in 1873. He has been written about by Nevada historians throughout the years; however, there had been limited information available. Since I had an up-close and personal perspective on this noted gunfighter, why didn't I know more about him? While growing up, I gazed down at his grave every time I looked out my living room window. How had I ignored his presence in my life and community for all these years?

Thus began my journey to uncover the full backstory of my silent neighbor who died on Main Street, Pioche, and is buried in "Boot Hill" with his boots on.

I now invite you to jump aboard and follow my journey, as I worked feverishly to confirm or deny Morgan Courtney's whereabouts as he navigated his way around the globe from his birth in southwest Ireland in 1842, to his death in Pioche in 1873.

My first step was to get to know Morgan Courtney better. I read everything about him that I could find in books and in newspapers. It was reported that he was born in Cahersiveen, County Kerry, Ireland in the 1840's, so that seemed to be a good place to start. I began a serious search using Ancestery.com looking for clues as to his birth parents, or any other relatives — to no avail. Eventually, I hired "Eneclann," a professional genealogical service in Dublin. As I awaited their final report, which was delayed due to Covid, a random thought occurred to me which went like this:

> I know for a fact from newspaper articles that Morgan Courtney was indicted and tried in court on a murder charge after a Main Street shootout which had started in one of the nearby saloons. Could some type of transcript from this trial possibly exist in the basement of the Lincoln County Courthouse

— the Courthouse where my dad practiced law while I was growing up?

The County Clerk's office told me that they did have some records from the 1800's. I dared not be optimistic — what were the chances? A couple of days later I received a call that they had the transcript, but due to its length, the cost would be $129 for the full copy. What they didn't know is that I would have mortgaged my house to get that transcript, as by this time I was seriously invested in the pursuit of this gunfighter.

Within a week, I received the 200-page, legal-size document written in the most stylized, curly handwritten script that you can imagine — almost unreadable. I started to panic, but after practicing for days I finally got the hang of it. Now I had the exact words of Morgan Courtney and a whole lot of other Pioche folks who were hanging around on Main Street the day Sullivan was shot.

I then realized that all I had to do to trace Courtney's steps was to follow the clues given in the transcript. What a ride!

Contents

Part I Morgan Courtney

Gunfighter

The Conductor, the Messengers,

and the Whip

"Last call; stage leaving Salt Lake City for Palisade, Eureka, Hamilton and Pioche," barked the Whip. "Stage leaving at 6:00 A.M. sharp."

In 1847, Brigham Young declared Salt Lake City, Utah, as the best place for his followers to establish new lives and worship as they wished without governmental interference. This location also happened to be the crossroads for most of the westward bound travelers on their way to Oregon or the California gold rush, so Salt Lake City quickly became a vital trading point for speculators and prospectors. Also, rich ore had been discovered in the Wasatch mountains just north of Salt Lake, so when the First Continental Railroad was completed at Promontory Summit in 1869, Salt Lake became a major transportation hub for every type of commerce, including mining and banking. The last train tracks on the section from Salt Lake City to Elko, Nevada, were placed Dec. 24, 1869.

However, in 1870, if you wanted to travel south to Pioche from Elko, your transportation choices for this journey would be stagecoach, horseback, or shoe leather; and given these choices, I would vote for a stagecoach, even as noisy, dirty, and bumpy as they were!

The final preparations were made for the stagecoach journey from Elko. The Conductor checked in the mail bags, and coin boxes, and took his place next to the Whip, the driver in charge of the full operation and safety of the passengers and cargo. The groom inspected the collars and harnesses of the team of six horses, directing his approval to the Whip.

The conveyance was a "Concord" stagecoach — top of the line, used almost ubiquitously across the Western frontier. The stages were meant for transporting coin for payroll, some bullion in the form of gold or silver bars, mail, and six to eight passengers. Larger items would be sent by heavy duty freight wagons.

By 1866, Wells Fargo had purchased most of the stage lines across the west creating a transportation monopoly. Since they were financially responsible for any lost cargo, the company found it necessary to employ armed guards (many times, two per coach) to guarantee the safety of the coin, the mail, and the passengers. Wells Fargo also employed a team of investigators, who worked in cooperation with local, state, and federal authorities regarding robbery cases — a constant threat. Author, Tom Clavin, noted, "Wells Fargo followed the money, and robbers followed Wells Fargo."[1] The six passengers took their places inside the coach — one of them a nice-looking, well-dressed Irishman, maybe late in his 20's. The Whip hollered at his team of horses, "Giddy ---up! Gee! Giddy---up! Gee!" and they were off down the dirt road to Palisades and Eureka.

The two gunmen with shotguns or "scatterguns" took their places on top of the stage, one on each side, behind the Whip and the Conductor. Scatterguns were used widely by the gunmen, as they could better hit a target, even if their aim was bad—good insurance while riding a bumpy conveyance and trying to hit a target on a moving horse—not an easy job, for sure! These gunmen were often referred to as "messengers."

The destination of the nattily-dressed young Irishman was Pioche — a journey of about 320 miles.

The average stagecoach, barring a broken wagon wheel, a snowstorm, lame horse, or armed robbery, could cover 60 to 70 miles per day; however, the teams of horses had to be replaced every 10 to 15 miles. This occurred at a station that consisted of a small building, stables and one station manager. These stations were placed the same distance apart along every route. If the passengers needed a break, they would have 10 to 15 minutes every 10 to 15 miles — no exception. These coaches had deadlines, and the station managers were highly efficient in replacing the teams of horses within this time frame. The team that had just been dropped off would then replace a team going the opposite direction upon its arrival. This way, each team of horses became totally attuned and comfortable with the same ten-to-fifteen-mile route that they took coming and going. Therefore, the trip from Salt Lake City to Pioche was about a three-and-a-half-day journey, as the coaches travelled through the night, weather and moonlight permitting, with regular stops to change horses.

Giddy...up! — Haw! The horses had been replaced with a fresh team in Palisades and the coach loaded with its travelling band was again rolling toward Eureka. The passengers were now comfortable with one another — the six passengers, the Conductor, the two Messengers and the Whip. The passengers were practicing appropriate stagecoach etiquette: you must sleep sitting straight up. Do not let your head rest on the shoulder of another passenger. Do not light up your pipe unless you are seated downwind. Foul language must never be used, nor off color jokes. It's best to avoid discussions of religion or politics with fellow passengers. And each person's knees must be laced between the knees of the passenger sitting on the opposite side of the coach.

The traveling band had, so far, made the trip without incident, but would need a fresh team of horses in Hamilton, and they were eagerly awaiting a hot dinner at the next stop in White Pine (now Ely, Nevada.) This would be the last major station before reaching Pioche, a twelve-hour journey from White Pine. Though the Central Pacific Railroad from Salt Lake City to Elko had been completed, access to the Eastern Nevada mines would remain dependent on the stagecoach for years to come.

The young Irish passenger enjoyed the stop at White Pine where he ran into an old friend, John Manning, a fellow miner, and Irish immigrant.

Gunfighters Ride Into Town

Meanwhile, our Wells Fargo stagecoach team of horses pulled hard against their collars to make the grade to the top of the road leading into the already infamous town of Pioche, Nevada.

Giddy...up! Gee! The stage veered right onto Main Street and pulled into the Wells Fargo yard at the south end of town, directly below the rich silver mining operations.

The noise of the blasting in the mines mingled with the sounds of people wandering in and out of the saloons and chop houses (steak restaurants), along with the sounds of wholesalers delivering their goods to the businesses along Main and Meadow Valley Streets.

The Whip directed the stage into the Wells Fargo depot. The two Messengers jumped down from their post, and the Conductor assisted the passengers from the coach and began unloading the mail and boxes of coin to be delivered to the mine owners for payroll. The Whip passed the reins of the team to the Pioche station attendant and wandered up Meadow Valley Street looking for a cool, well-deserved beverage.

The handsome, well-dressed, young Irishman disembarked from the coach and collected a small satchel from the conductor. He appeared to be quiet, reserved, and good-natured.

His name was Morgan Courtney.

Colt 44 And A "Henry"

When Morgan Courtney stepped off that Wells Fargo stagecoach and headed to the Hotel to order a six shooter and a Henry rifle to be sent from Salt Lake City, everyone in town soon knew about it. It was an event worth whispering about, and because of this, Charles Gracey, an employee of one of the mines, heard of it, and, thankfully, lived to write about it. Even as wild as Pioche was, no ordinary citizen needed a Henry rifle. First off, they were very expensive. The 44-caliber Henry went for $40 ($804 today). Secondly, the gun was designed by Benjamin Tyler Henry as a weapon of war, and most were sold to the Union army. Personal weapons were allowed on a Wells Fargo stagecoach, but I'm not sure about a Henry rifle.

The average man in the West at that time would have a shotgun for shooting rabbits, deer, and wild birds. A pistol was not considered necessary, and a Henry rifle which carried 17 rounds of ammunition was completely out of the question. Anyone with a Henry rifle was preparing for a battle with a large band of hostile Indians, or to protect or steal cattle, or to protect or confiscate private property. In other words, the need for a Henry had to be for an intricately planned war-like engagement.

Confederate Colonel, John Mosby, noted, "That damned Yankee rifle that can be loaded on Sunday and fired all week." Some Union soldiers would use their reenlistment bonus to purchase a Henry rifle, as they felt it may very well save their life.

Therefore, in 1870, when a man ordered his Henry rifle from Salt Lake City it was crystal clear to everyone in town that he was a gunfighter and had arrived to go to work. When a gentleman arrived with a Henry *and* an 1860 Colt Army 44 pistol there was just no room for any doubt as to his intentions.

In 1870, a Colt 44 cost $14.50 ($291 today) and an ordinary pistol that could be purchased at the local hardware store would cost about $6.00. So, Morgan Courtney was sporting over $1,000 (today's dollars) in professional weapons and a very fancy wardrobe. I think that we can safely deduce that this was not his first job as a gunfighter, and that he had purposely been sent for by mine owners.

At about the same time, probably September or October of 1870, three other polite, gentlemanly fellows, all under the age of 30, showed up at Bullionville, south of Pioche—the place where the ore from Treasure Hill was hauled for processing prior to the journey to Salt Lake City for sale. The three gentlemen were Michael Casey, Barney Flood and William Bethers. None of these three men nor Morgan Courtney were known to anyone in Pioche, and their appearance was not that of the typical miner. They didn't fit the miner's profile and were, therefore, a hot topic for discussion among the locals.

In the Fall of 1870, there were two operational mines on Treasure Hill which were running successfully and paying dividends — the Meadow Valley Company in which F.L.A. Pioche was a major investor and the

Raymond and Ely mine, owned by W. H. Raymond and John Ely.

One year prior to this, both mines were struggling with methods to remove the proven ore from the ground, to process or "smelt" it, and to safely transport the refined ore to market. Smelting the ore required a furnace, and furnaces require charcoal and men who were capable of running and maintaining the machinery. This is a process in which intense heat along with the introduction of mercury is used to separate the fine ore (the gold and silver) from the rocky material which surrounds it, called the "gangue." The goal is to be able to smelt the ore, extract the fine minerals from the gangue at the nearest location possible to the mine, and ship only the refined mineral to the market—in this case Salt Lake City, Utah.

Fortunately for the Raymond and Ely mine owners, a young mining engineer, Charles Gracey, had recently found his way to Pioche, reaching out to new territory in hopes of getting in on the ground floor of a new strike — and that he did. Gracey, raised in Michigan, had trained as a blacksmith in his youth before moving to California in 1866, and then followed mining strikes to Elko, White Pine, and ultimately Pioche, Nevada.

In Pioche, Gracey soon met the mining entrepreneurs, W.H. Raymond, and John Ely, who needed a blacksmith. They had determined that their best chances of purchasing the specific, carefully chosen Pioche mine, was to tear down a five-stamp smelter that they owned in Pahranagat Valley (now

Alamo, Nevada) and move it to Bullionville, south of Pioche, to process ore near the mine. (A stamp is a heavy metal rod which is pushed up and down by a battering arm, pulverizing the rock taken out of the ground, so that the valuable ore can be separated from the useless rock, the tailings.)

They were sure if they could get the mill moved to the correct location, that they would then be able to attract investors and purchase the mine in question. At that point it would be a risk worth taking for the investors. Gracey agreed to move this mill, which was close to 100 miles south, a huge undertaking, for "grub only" in hopes that the owners could indeed purchase the mine, hit a big strike, and pay the investors. All this represented a big financial risk for everyone involved.

"For grub only" means that he had agreed to work for no payment, other than his food and supplies. Whoa! Charles Gracey now had the chance he was waiting for to get in on the beginning of a large operation. Several other men took the same offer to work "for grub" and built the road to the relocated mill.

Gracey, a very talented guy, was able to get the mill running by January in 1870. Mr. Raymond came to look at the first amalgam, pinched it and said, "That is good; it squeaks. Gold and silver are the only ones that will squeak."[2] Game on!

The ore was worth $300 per ton ($6,033 today), and in sixty days Raymond and Ely paid all their debts and had struck it rich! Charles Gracey became their chief engineer for the next seven years, during which time the mine grew to running sixty stamps. This was an enormous operation, putting Pioche on the map, resulting in a population tsunami and the beginning of a decade of violence.

Luckily, Charles Gracey lived to a ripe old age and recorded many of his recollections for the Nevada State Historical Society published in 1908. From him we have an eyewitness account of the claim jumping battle which ensued on the Raymond and Ely claim. Gracey was an engineer for the mine, and he was in a position to know all the major players, like Morgan Courtney, and the three other noted gentlemen who had recently arrived in Pioche.

Gracey reports that the trouble started when two brothers, Tom and Frank Newland, opened a mine above the Washington and Creole—a mine that Raymond and Ely had purchased as a buffer claim to tie up the ground next to their new, "strike-it-rich" producing mine. The Newlands requested permission from Raymond and Ely to run a tunnel through the Washington and Creole to hook up with the existing tunnel above their working mine. This would enable them to avoid digging a shaft and reduce their costs.

Raymond and Ely agreed, because the buffer ground they would be tunneling through was thought to be of no value, and they wanted to be good neighbors on "the Hill." The Newland brothers started digging the tunnel, but upon reaching the Washington and Creole, they exposed a nine-foot ledge of very rich ore — $300 per ton. What to do?

The brothers negotiated with Raymond and Ely who gave them permission to work the ledge for 30 days

— a most generous deal. Mr. Raymond was pleased saying, "That ore might have lain there for years or might never have been found."[3]   But, when it was time for the Newland brothers to vacate the ledge and return to their own ground after the agreed upon 30 days, they refused to do so. In fact, they hired a team of watchmen (messengers or gunmen) from White Pine, Nevada, who quickly built a fort around the entrance to the valuable ledge, and the brothers continued mining as rapidly as possible, taking their ore to Silver Peak (near Tonopah, Nevada) for processing. (Today, Silver Peak, Nevada is the location of a large lithium producing operation.)

Sheriff John Kane was contacted and walked up to the mine intending to enforce the law by ordering the Newland brothers to vacate the Raymond and Ely tunnel, but when faced with the gunmen, he was forced to retreat. The Newland brothers, completely overtaken by gold fever, warned Raymond and Ely that, "If either of them set foot in camp, it would be a certain death."[4]

Enter Morgan Courtney, the dapper young Irishman, recently arrived from Salt Lake City; who had received shipment of his Henry rifle and six-shooter pistol; and who was conveniently acquainted with the three polite young men who had just moved to Pioche — Michael Casey, Barney Flood, and William Bethers. Did these four young men know each other from another place, or was it pure coincidence that they showed up in Pioche at about the same time as Courtney? According to author, Charles Convis, Morgan Courtney had an agreement with the mine owners, and had hired the other three men to take the Raymond and Ely protection job.

The foursome, who according to Gracey, appeared to be led by Morgan Courtney, met with Raymond and Ely and made an offer, "We will drive those fellows off, if you will give us a written promise that we can have the ground for 30 days."[5] The two mine owners were up against it. They could not turn to the law for protection —Sheriff Kane had already tried to enforce the law and couldn't. They had no other alternative but to take the "Courtney and crew" offer to rid the mine owners of the unrightful claim jumpers, the "Newland brothers."

The clandestine foursome kept to themselves for a month or two, until the night of November 8, 1870, when they arranged for a case of whiskey (with no return address) to be delivered to the Newland camp. The foursome was hiding in a large grove of pine trees above the armed fortress surrounding the tunnel in question. The Newland gunmen took the bait, drank the whiskey, and proceeded to get good and drunk. At 3:00 a.m. the Courtney gang stormed down the hill from the pine grove with guns blazing and drove the Newland gunmen out. One man, W. G. Snell, was killed in the process, and several others were wounded. Courtney received a slight, but not serious, wound. W. G. Snell was #10 in Pioche to be buried in the Boot Hill Cemetery.

Raymond and Ely kept their word, and the Courtney crew mined the Washington and Creole ground for 30 days, netting each of the four gunmen, $15,000 ($301,500 today). Charles Gracey felt that this was the beginning of the major violence in Pioche, as within the next few years there were at least seven men killed over mining claim disputes.

Regarding Morgan Courtney, Gracey states this opinion, "Morgan Courtney turned out to be a sport and was counted 'chief' of the fighting men. He gambled very heavily."[6]

Guns And Grudges

Barney Flood, one of the four successful gunmen, was later indicted for participating in the stabbing of another local, Thomas Coleman, but was released due to lack of evidence. Michael Casey, while on his way to the bank to deposit his $15,000 pay off, ran into one of his debtors (Gorson) and immediately got into a fight. He agreed to pay Gorson what he owed, $100; but then the two started fighting over the amount of interest. Casey shot and wounded Gorson, who died the next day. However, before he died, Gorson willed $5,000 to the man who would kill Casey — a decision which would eventually lead to even more violence.

In time, Casey, a man of little forethought, then managed to provoke Jim Levy, a friend of Gorson, who happened to be an eyewitness to his death. This was an unfortunate move on the part of Casey, because Jim Leavy took this opportunity to shoot Casey on Main Street and collect the $5,000 reward left by Gorson.

Bill Bethers died about a year later—one account reported was that he died in a gunfight in Eureka. In time, Morgan Courtney, who was charged with the murder of Snell, but was released, became sole survivor of the Newland Mine shoot out. Gorson was #19 buried in the Boot Hill Cemetery, and Michael Casey was #21.

Now, unfortunately, according to the engineer Charles Gracey, Casey's remaining friends were enemies of Levy who with his new money and "fastest gun in town" reputation changed from a miner to a fearless gunfighter, and left Pioche to expand his horizons in other lawless towns in the West. He ended up in Tombstone, Arizona, around the time of the O.K. Corral shootout. There was still no law in Pioche, and the grudge matches continued, fueled by unlimited alcohol, prostitutes, guns and easy money.

In Pioche in the 1860's and 70's, "Law and Order" looked like this:

> —J.E. Matthews was the first Sheriff appointed in 1867 and resigned on July 27, 1868
>
> —William Ritter was elected Nov. 3, 1868, and resigned on November 21, 1868 (it was a long three weeks!)
>
> —John Kane served from 1870 to 1872.
>
> —W.S. Travis served 1872 to 1874.

The length of service was improving, but didn't get much better until the 1880's.

Kane, a miner prior to becoming sheriff, dealt with the situation the best he could by appointing large numbers of deputies. In fact, it became the custom in Pioche to pin a badge on the worst desperados and let them pick each other off as fast as possible. "It was a cheap method of outlaw control and kept the ordinary folks out of the fray."[7]

Local Pioche historians describe these early lawmen:

> "Exuberant and daring lawmen that fitted the
> life and times of Lincoln County. Some
> eyeballed the womenfolk a bit too often.
> Others were more interested in county funds.
> One went to prison for a few years, and yet
> another ended up running the State prison.
> One whipped a man through the town streets
> – another drank himself to death in office.
> There were sheriffs that never packed a gun.
> Others would shoot anything that moved."[8]

As remote as Pioche was from any other metropolis,
its reputation for lawlessness had spread like wildfire.
The lawmen were outnumbered and out gunned by
the lawless.

Pioche quickly grew to a population of about 1,000
regardless of the violence, and now included 114
children. One unidentified observer known only as
A.H.R. reports,

> "Since my last visit to this place the town has
> improved greatly in appearance. The canvas
> houses have been removed and good
> substantial wooden structures erected in their
> place, giving the place a much better
> appearance…. the stores present a busy
> appearance, and all the branches of trade are
> in the hands of good enterprising men."[9]

Where Is Pioche, Anyway?

The town of Pioche is located about halfway down the mountain from the entrance to some of the most prosperous mines located on the famous Treasure Hill. Silver had been discovered there by a Paiute Indian in 1863, who took samples to a Mormon Scout, William Hamblin. The samples taken by Hamblin to Salt Lake City proved the value of the ore, but not much mining occurred until 1868, due to the claim's remote location — no roads; no railroads; lots of hazards.

Pioche is 429 miles east of Reno, 320 miles southwest of Salt Lake City, and in 1864, the land directly south was occupied only by native American tribes. The costs of setting up a mine and then delivering the ore to Salt Lake City for distribution were prohibitive. However, wherever the promise of a "Mother lode" of riches appears, as sure as rain, a financier will follow. Meet Francois Louis Alfred Pioche, born in 1818 in France, educated as a lawyer — a man who had recently inherited 100,000 francs from a rich uncle. As they say in France, "Voila!"

Monsieur Pioche first traveled to Chile looking for adventure, then to the California gold rush in 1849. After hearing about the silver strike in eastern Nevada, he set sail to France to procure investors, and successfully returned to San Francisco with six million dollars for investment in the American West.

Voila! Voila! The newly discovered mine on Treasure Hill received the needed funds to become operational, and F.L.A. Pioche now had a town named after him. One small problem: the miners, businessmen, and other citizens of Pioche had no instruction in pronunciation of French words, so they pronounced the name of their town as "Pioche" with "ch" sound like "couch"; instead of the French pronunciation of "Peoshe," with a soft "sh" sound like "shoe," and the former pronunciation stuck.

Unfortunately, in 1872, F.L.A. Pioche took his own life. He did not leave a suicide note, so his reasoning remains a mystery to this day.

In the meantime, miners from all points on the globe rode on carts or walked hundreds of miles to reach Pioche—the newest "promised land". They were followed quickly by financial speculators of the best and worst kind, and by merchants, carpenters, teamsters, saloonkeepers, a few dancing girls, and unchaperoned ladies looking for adventure and some extra coin.

All the mines were closely nestled together on Treasure Hill, which meant that the tunnels drilled and dug out by the mine owners were exceedingly close to one another and could easily intersect. And intersect, they did, resulting in legal battles and physical altercations of the most serious nature — some ending in deaths. In fact, the Federal Mining law of 1872, still in effect today, can be attributed to the Pioche problem. This law defines the right to follow mineral veins through claims staked by another person. The presence of legal teams to enforce these laws eventually followed the mining boom towns, but their effectiveness was a painstaking process which took time. In the meantime, chaos ensued.

The Pioche mine owners were in a difficult position considering the fact they were investing hard-earned money or had leveraged high-risk loans on a mining venture in a remote and lawless western territory, driven by silver and gold-laced illusions of becoming filthy rich. The only remedy for protecting their investment was to hire professional gunfighters as security guards at their mines to prevent others from sabotaging, thieving, or taking over their operations by force, known as "claim jumping."

Luckily for the Pioche mine owners, they were not alone. There were mine owners with remote, unprotected mines by the thousands, all over Colorado, Idaho, Montana and Utah as well as Nevada needing protection, and a whole industry of professional gunmen had appeared to fill the need. This was one opportunity for Irish immigrants who had difficulty getting jobs on the east coast. Many found their way west to the gold and silver fields, and offering protection was another avenue to a larger payday.

The Civil War ended in 1865, leaving thousands of restless soldiers loose to re-establish their lives, and most of them had been trained to handle a rifle. Many would return to family farms and businesses, marry, and continue life as they had known it before the war; but there would be a percentage of soldiers who would strike out for the West to try something new. After the war ended, the government saw no need to store a huge arsenal of weapons, so this abundant supply of rifles and pistols was then sold to soldiers and the general public. The wild west would become more dangerous as these weapons were released. They seemed to move like lightning across the prairie to Texas, and then to every gold rush town along the Sierra Nevada and the Rockies.

Life In 1870's Pioche

Historian, James Hulse, noted in "The Nevada Adventure" that Pioche was born on the upside of a generous bubble which unfortunately burst after four years. This is mainly the case of most gold and silver mining bonanzas in the West. These towns were thrown together faster than a game of pick-up sticks because its citizens knew they would probably leave in five years. The game is how fast can we extract these precious metals, walk away with a fat payday, and move back to where we came from — or move to a fancier place like Sacramento or San Francisco.

In the meantime, according to the 1870 census, the population of Pioche had exploded into a town of 1144 souls, and the demographics are fascinating. The places of birth ranged from Denmark, England, Ireland, Scotland, Wales, and to Utah and China.

According to the 1870 Census, of the 1144 total population, 268 of them were women and 876 men. 178 were under the age of 10; six people were in their 60's, none in their 70's and one person was 81 years old. Of the women over age 18, four were hurdy dancers, one milliner, one 65-year-old "keeping a hotel," and the rest were "at home keeping house."

The occupations of the men were as follows:

Laborer—69	Lawyer—6
Livery—5	M.D.—2
Mill—8	Miner—365
Prospector—4	Silver Miner—24
Teamster—61	Wood Chopper—4
Farmer—58	

There is very little actual farmland around Pioche, but there were ranchers running cattle, raising chickens and hay who were probably all lumped into the "farmer" category. Also, the "silver miners" should have been included as "miners," as this was the primary metal being extracted.

Life for the women in mining camps had to be beyond tough. Author, RaNae Travers notes, "The early mining camps essentially attracted two types of women: Married women following their husbands and young women planning to make their living as prostitutes." I, personally, don't know which group had it worse – neither were good options.

The streets of Pioche were dusty and dirty during the dry months and wet and muddy during the winter. There was no running water; no stream; no lake; and no river — just dirt and mud. The women were trying to "keep house," but how?

The *Pioche Daily Record* described the town during spring run-off, "The mud is becoming a serious impediment to travel by vehicle, on horseback, or on foot. There is a reeking mass of rubbish, decaying refuse, and offensive decaying matters."

The women, for the most part, were living with their families in small one or two room cabins with no insulation, no running water, but hopefully a wood stove. Sanitation would have been close to impossible, and how in the world would you keep your children healthy under these circumstances? The husbands had a vision of mining for silver, making enough money to move on to a much better life, and their wives obediently followed, hoping the dream would become a reality. For most, that was not the result of the sacrifices.

On the brighter side, businesses were popping up on both sides of the main street, and a regular society was taking shape. St. John's Masonic lodge was built in 1869, and the Odd Fellows and Rebeka's Lodge in 1872. Most members carried guns, which were hung on pegs during the formal meetings. The Pioche Hotel, a boarding house for the single men, was constructed in the late 1860's and is standing today.

In 1870, Father Scanlon was sent from the Archdiocese of San Francisco to Pioche to build a church and a hospital. That same year Ozi Whitaker, a newly ordained minister of the Episcopal Church, arrived to hopefully plant a church in Pioche. He was known as a charismatic speaker and was also very creative with making do when circumstances were challenging. He held his first service in one of the saloons where, almost 150 persons had packed the saloon to capacity while a crowed gathered outside in the street due to lack of lack of space in the building.

Unfortunately, during a very dry day in September of 1871, a great fire broke out leveling ten stores, six to eight restaurants, all the bars, five lodging houses and four law offices. 2,000 people were left homeless. In 1871, water had to be hauled four miles and the volunteer fire company of 40 members had no equipment, which turned this fire into a total disaster.

Amazingly, these tough and stalwart citizens refused to let go of their dreams, and the town was rebuilt in six months, proving to be more progressive than before. It is reported that at some point after the fire, the town boasted 37 bars and 25 houses of ill repute. Some of the bars that advertised in the local newspaper were:

John C. Lynch, Fashion Saloon and Club Room,

Meadow Valley Brewery, H.D. Bonners,

Buckeye Saloon, Occidental,

City Club Room, Hamilton's,

Palace Club, and the Philadelphia Brewer

The gunfighters created much of the excitement along Main and Meadow Valley Streets, as we have seen by following Morgan Courtney. However, there were additional interesting characters populating these streets who should not go unnoticed.

Casual Evening With The "Roughs"

The Newland Mine shootout had occurred on November 8, 1870, resulting in the huge payoff of $15,000 per gunman, so Morgan Courtney and Barney Flood had no real need to ever work again. However, Pioche was a place of much action and possibilities. Perhaps they envisioned discovering and operating their own mine in the near future?

In the meantime, the two men had time on their hands and were in the habit of spending many evenings gambling and drinking in the local saloons. So, three months later, on the night of February 22, 1871, Morgan Courtney, Barney Flood and Michael Dolan were out for the evening. Of course, Courtney and Flood were flush with $15,000 in cash from the Washington and Creole Mine shootout.

A gentleman known as Thomas Coleman, now the duly appointed Marshall in nearby Treasure City, about 100 miles north of Pioche, was in town visiting a woman named Sophie. Some sources report that Coleman invited Courtney, Flood, and Dolan to his residence for drinks, and other sources reported they were in a brothel. It is presumed that they must have known each other at a prior time and place, because they started fighting over a woman—and possibly prior grudges, which resulted in the brutal stabbing of Thomas Coleman. He did not die immediately, but did, in fact, pass away as a direct result of the injuries sustained. He was stabbed five times, and there were three other men in the room—so who did it?

Courtney was arrested and bail was set at $6,000. Later Barney Flood was arrested as well, but the case against both men was dropped due to a lack of evidence. According to the *Gold Hill News* of Feb. 27, 1871, "Coleman was well known in Sacramento ten years ago, as the last of fifteen roughs or fighters belonging to that city, all of whom died violent deaths." Newspapers in Gold Hill and in Idaho City mention Coleman as being in Virginia City at one time as well as in Idaho City. It was not unusual in Nevada or in other mining states for a noted gunman to be later hired as a Sheriff or a deputy — many times in the same towns where they had committed crimes. Thomas Coleman was a perfect example of a known gunman, known as a "rough" in Sacramento, who was hired in Nevada as a Marshall. The towns were doing the best they could to keep peace, and to make this happen, a close examination of a person's past was just not feasible.

Virginia City and Idaho City were both places that Courtney had previously been, as well. Obviously bad blood had developed between Coleman and at least one of the other two men prior to the meeting in Pioche. However, what were the chances that Courtney, Flood or Dolan were going to testify against the other? It was a small world in the 1870's. None of the three assailants were brought to trial — all three were let go for lack of evidence. Thomas Coleman was the 18th person to be buried in the Boot Hill Cemetery. As mentioned before, the sheriffs in Pioche knew that "given a little time, the roughs will pick each other off and save the town the cost of a trial."[10]

Scott Vs. Courtney

Morgan Courtney was now a saloon crowd hero, despite the Thomas Coleman knife fight, and evidently the saloon crowd was a sizeable one. He had won a planned and pitched battle for the Raymond and Ely mine owners who were well respected in Pioche, putting him on the right side of justice in that instance. He was now a "big man" in town, referred to as "Chief," with a boat load of money that he spent freely in the saloons, the brothels, and at the gambling tables.

Our Irish man-about-town was also a veritable fashion plate. "He prided himself on ordering suits of the finest, black broadcloth, and shirts of the purest, white linen, all decorated with the most expensive jewelry. He also had his fingernails manicured."[11]   In fact, he dressed much better than most of the mine owners.

Mark Twain in *"Roughing It"* describes the Virginia City gunfighters as follows: "The desperado stalked the streets with a swagger graded according to the number of his homicides, and a nod of recognition from him was sufficient to make a humble admirer happy for the rest of the day. The deference that was paid to a desperado of wide reputation, and 'kept his private graveyard,' as the phrase went, was marked, and cheerfully accorded. When he moved along the sidewalk in his excessively long-tailed frock-coat, shiny stump-toed boots, and with dainty little slouch hat tipped over left eye, the small-fry roughs made room for his majesty; when he entered the restaurant, the waiters deserted banker and merchants to overwhelm him with obsequious service; when he shouldered his way to a bar, the shouldered parties wheeled indignantly, recognized him and apologized."[12]

Morgan Courtney had adopted the persona of a Nevada gunfighter and was willing to live the part he had chosen. Pioche was his new home, and he was getting the attention and the deference that he had desired for a long time.

Multiple sources say that Morgan Courtney was a gambler, in a very big way, and his game of choice was Faro. In the 1870's, miners on every continent played the game, and they played it for long hours and with much vigor. In fact, in 1881, Wyatt Earp, who had an interest in the upscale Oriental Saloon in Tombstone, also dealt the Faro game there—a very lucrative enterprise for the Saloon.

Faro originated in France in the 17th century. It was a fast-moving casino game for two or more players. All that is needed for play is a green cloth, painted with a suit of spades arranged in a horseshoe, a small box containing one deck of cards (a dealer's box), and a card tracking device called a "case keeper." Bettors would then place bets on the rank of the cards as they were dealt. Unfortunately, Faro could be rigged by using a manipulated dealer's box, enabling the dealer to slip out two cards at a time. It is rumored that Wyatt Earp was a specialist in marking cards used in his Faro games.

Morgan Courtney loved to gamble, and he was hooked on Faro. It's not known if he was a particularly good gambler, but it appears that he, for sure, thought he was — after all, he was the 'Chief' in one of the toughest towns in the West!

In April of 1871, just five months after earning $15,000 saving the Washington and Creole mine for mine owners Raymond and Ely, and weeks after being released from jail after the knifing murder of Thomas Coleman, Courtney entered the public gambling room in the boarding house of M. McClusky in Pioche, where a Faro game was in process with Russell Scott dealing. Scott had obtained a license from the County of Lincoln to operate Faro games.

Courtney proceeded to lose $600 that night and did not have the cash to pay the debt to the dealer, but he promised that he could pay it in a couple of days. He did repay the loan as promised, but not in full—he was $100 short. Regardless of this, Scott allowed Courtney to enter the game again a few nights later, feeling sure that Courtney was good for the money, and he allowed him to gamble on credit. Courtney then lost $2,000 that night, plus he still owed the "house" $100 from the prior night. This amounted to $42,231 in today's dollars—a huge debt.

Why, I ask, was Courtney gambling on credit when he struck it rich just five months previously to the tune of $301,650 in today's dollars? Where was the money? If our Irish vagabond was willing to gamble more than $40,000 in today's money in one night and risk losing it, maybe he could easily have lost all his money in five months, but there is little evidence of what happened to his money. However, The *Elko Independent*, Feb. 4, 1871, did report that Raymond and Ely Company had shipped bullion amounting to $13,156.07, and Morgan Courtney, Flood and others shipped five gold bars valued at $8,941. This shipment most likely was sent to Salt Lake City to be processed into script (spendable cash.) This was the central processing and banking location for most of the mining towns in the contiguous States.

In the meantime, Russell Scott was not at all amused or impressed by Morgan Courtney, and he filed suit against him in the local Lincoln County court to recover the sizeable debt. Scott lost the case, but he was not done with Morgan Courtney. He immediately appealed to the Nevada Supreme Court.

Morgan Courtney had been in Pioche for less than one year and had already been involved with the death of two men, W. B. Snell and Thomas Coleman, and is the now the defendant in a gambling case being heard in the Nevada Supreme Court — quite a record for an Irish immigrant in his 20's. These gunfighters, with their firearms and swagger, earning such large sums of money in mining communities must have been noticed by all. Miners made $4.00 per day, which was considered high wages, but gunfighters were making $20 per day.

The Nevada Supreme Court heard this case in January of 1872, and voted to uphold the lower court's ruling. They determined that Mr. Scott's license issued by Lincoln County was strictly to protect him from being prosecuted criminally for running an illegal gambling business, as gambling was, in fact, illegal in Nevada at that time, as it was in every other State. The license did not give him the right to collect bad debts, but only to run a gambling game free of prosecution by the State of Nevada. Russell Scott was out of luck this time, and Morgan Courtney, once again, got away with his wild card. Oh, the luck of the Irish!

Part II Cahersiveen, Ireland "The Beginning"

What's In A Name?

It's an understandable question to ponder at this point, "How in the world does an Irish immigrant get to the western United States and end up in the remote mining camp of Pioche, Nevada, in 1870; and how did he get those expensive guns; and how did he become well known enough as a gunfighter to attract the attention of Mr. Raymond and Mr. Ely?"

Giddy... up — Haw! (a teamster's command to a team of horses to start moving and turn left.)

This story is going to make a sharp left turn. Hang on, please!

Morgan Courtney was, in fact, born Richard Moriarty, in Cahersiveen, County Kerry, Ireland, and I will refer to him to by his legal name while tracing him from Ireland to Nevada.

Let's go back to 1842 in Ireland and see if we can figure out who he really was, why he left Ireland, and what made him become a gunfighter in the American West.

Richard Moriarty was probably born late 1842 or early 1843. The Irish did not keep official birth records at that time. In their culture, the important date marking one's birth was the date of baptism in the Catholic Church, and most everyone was Catholic.

He was born in one of the most beautiful areas of Ireland. Cahersiveen is on the Atlantic coast near the Dingle Peninsula—a very popular area for today's tourists to hike the terrain near the cliffs and motor around the peninsula taking in the breathtaking scenery.

Moriarty is a common name in southwest Ireland and has always been associated with County Kerry. Modern statistics reveal that 90 percent of births registered with the name Moriarty occur in Kerry.

The name goes back to the 11th century and possibly further. The Irish or Gaelic spelling is O'Muirchearlaigh, but, of course, the name was recorded many other ways through the centuries.

The Moriarty's are of Celtic heritage. The Celts were the Iron Age settlers who first appeared in Ireland about 500 B.C. from Northern Europe. There were various Neolithic tribes there before that time, but the Celts defined the Irish traditions, religion, and culture. These traditions were always passed down orally, so the written language in Ireland developed slowly, creating a very well-preserved Gaelic language, spoken widely today in Ireland, as well as in Scotland, Cornwall, Breton, and Wales. In fact, this storytelling tradition is still "alive and well" in the Irish population today—you can find it in any pub in Ireland!

The Vikings had made a good attempt at conquering Ireland and had a large presence but were pushed out by the Celts at the battle of Clontarf in 1014. Next the Normans from northern France took a shot at occupation; however, after hundreds of years of

assimilation, they all became known as the Gaels—
and some say the Normans became more Irish than
the Irish.

Ireland, through all these occupations, remained
essentially independent until the 1500's, when they
were conquered by the English during the reign of
Henry the VIII, who declared himself King of
Ireland. In 1542 he dissolved the Monasteries, the
backbone of religious life in Ireland and a component
of the economy, as well. The next ten years saw
further encroachment by the British with increasingly
restrictive laws, which created a vast distinction
between the classes, setting the stage for many of the
conflicts in Ireland lasting until today.

The Irish Have Troubles

For some time, the agricultural economy of Ireland prospered due to the increased demand for grain from England. The population increased dramatically, but by the 1830's, the fertile soil was becoming depleted from over production, and productivity fell dramatically, combined with the partial failure of the potato crop in 1845, followed by a complete failure in 1846; a severe winter in 1847; and another potato crop failure in 1848. The result was that severe starvation and disease set in across the entire country, lasting into 1852.

Richard Moriarty was born at the beginning of this massive human disaster. From 1845 to 1851, Ireland lost a quarter of its population — one half of this number emigrated to England, America or Australia, and the other half perished.

Coln Toibin and Diarmaid Ferritor in their book, *The Irish Famine*, summed up the causes of famine, "It is now agreed, at least more or less, that around a million people died of diseases, hunger, and fever in the years between 1846 and 1849, and two million people emigrated. The west of Ireland suffered most, and there are people there today who claim to be haunted still by the silences, absences, and emptiness the Famine left."[13]

Mary Golden, of Cahersiveen, wrote her master's thesis in 1997, entitled, *"Aspects of Cahersiveen Town and Parish 1811-1867."* What a treasure trove—a thesis written about the exact small town where Richard Moriarty was born, and which covered the years of his birth and upbringing. From Ms. Golden's work, I was better able to understand exactly what had happened in this hard-hit area, and why it was affected to a greater degree than most other parts of Ireland.

Essentially, most of County Kerry is remote with a great deal of bogland—not suitable for successful agriculture. The English residents in Dublin, on the opposite side of the country, owned the land, and sublet to several large Protestant families, who, in turn, sublet again to the Irish O'Connell family.

The O'Connell's then sublet small parcels of land to their numerous Irish tenants. They charged high rent to these tenants in order to pay their rent to the Protestant landlords, who, in turn, had to pay rent to Trinity College in Dublin and make a profit themselves. The writing was on the wall—the landlords got richer and richer, and the tenants on the small parcels of bogland got poorer and poorer.

The tenants were very dependent on their potato crops, as the potato was one of the few crops which grew well near the coast. Other parts of Ireland which were more suited to agriculture fared better when the famine hit. There were few agricultural remedies for the population in the southwest area. The families were very attached to their small parcels of land, as their ancestors had lived on the same parcels for centuries— it was a clan mentality, which promoted sticking to traditional methods rather than trying new ways of supporting themselves.

The British were also dreadfully slow to implement helpful remedies; and, instead of trying to feed the starving population in place, they built large dormitories and pushed the starving families into these huge, crowded workhouses. Of course, typhus and other diseases then flourished killing more people, resulting in a vicious cycle of homelessness, illness, and death.

Tracing the family ancestry for Richard Moriarty through this period became very difficult. Many Parish records in these rural areas were lost, or burned in fires, as is the case of "workhouse" records. There are no records of the workhouse in Cahersiveen at all — none. Therefore, I am still trying to gain information about Richard and his family through local libraries, but it is tough going. Was his family able to stay in their home during the famine, or did they end up in a workhouse? If I can ever determine this, it will tell us a lot about Richard's developmental years, and perhaps explain some of his behaviors and decisions.

At least we know because of his birth location and year of birth, that he was brought into the world during one of the worst human crises ever recorded. The fact that he survived his childhood is a miracle, as many infants were dying every month during those years.

It is unfortunate that in the midst of the bounteous, God-given natural beauty of the Irish countryside, the

Irish people had to endure the worst of the worst tragedies. The result was that County Kerry had the highest annual rate of emigration in the country. The 1841 census showed a population as high as 295,000, and by 1911, the population was 160,000. Every family was broken up — members whisked away to all four corners of the globe, and most would never meet again.

During the 1840's, a socially aware American woman from Vermont, Asenath Nicholson, took it upon herself to travel to Ireland twice to see for herself what was happening; and to, perhaps, be able to report back to the States as to the condition of the people. Her second trip in 1847-1849, resulted in the book, "*Annals of the Famine in Ireland.*" Ms. Nicholson was able to mingle with Protestant and Catholic clergy, government workers, and common people as well, all over the Country, chronicling in her book her personal viewpoint of what she saw and heard. It's a book that is rough to digest, but so worth the trouble. I will quote some of her findings:

> "Coffins were now becoming scarce, and in the mountainous regions and islands, two rough boards, with the corpse in the rags which were about it when the breath departed, placed between these, and a straw rope wound about, was the coveted boon which clung to them to the last."[14]

> "I was directed to a respectable house to procure lodgings for a few days the disheartened widow said. Two days ago, I could have given you a well-furnished

bedroom and parlor, but now I have neither table, chair, nor carpet on the floors; the money was demanded for a new tax just levied. I could not raise it, my furniture was taken, and I have no means to fetch it back, or to get bread."

"I have been here many years, and have seen the workings and effects of a poorhouse, and can only say – the best that can be said of them – they are prisons under a different name, calculated to produce a principle of idleness, and to degrade, never to elevate, to deaden in the human heart that rational self-respect which individual support generates and which should be kept up; and may I never be doomed to die in a poorhouse."

"A cabin was seen closed one day a little out of the town, when a man had the curiosity to open it, and in a dark corner he found a family of the father, mother, and two children, lying in close compact. The father was considerably decomposed; the mother, it appeared, had died last..."

As difficult as it is to read, I have placed these quotes one after another for a reason. I felt that they needed to be read this way in order to really understand the magnitude of this event in the world's history.

If Richard Moriarty was born in 1842 or early 1843, he would have been four years old at the beginning of the worst part of the famine and nine or ten at the end. Ireland would be negatively affected for decades to come, as were most families.

My one remaining clue as to the whereabouts of Richard Moriarty while he was in Ireland came from this Police Record:

Name: Richard Moriarty

Birthdate: 1842

Admission Date: 15 Feb 1858

Admission Place: Kerry, Ireland

Charge: Absconding from his Master

Jail: Tralee

Identification No.: 133

There is no absolute proof that this is our guy, but it's a pretty good fit, as mass emigration was occurring during this time, especially from Southwest Ireland. At age 16, Richard would have been considered emancipated, and it was a good possibility that the Court mandated him to emigrate to Australia, especially if his parents could not be found, or were not able to feed or, perhaps, control him. A majority of the Irish from County Kerry who emigrated during the 1850's, chose to locate in Australia, rather than America.

There are no remaining records pertaining to Identification Number 133 — no narrative as to what the sentence was or what happened. Once again, there is nothing to conclusively hang our hat on. Most of the "convict" ships to Australia had sailed prior to the 1850's. However, Australia was still offering bonus money to the ship owners to bring laborers to their country. Also, sometimes the Irish

Government would pay the ships' owners to transport targeted persons for emigration — like miners or domestic servants.

We do know for sure that Richard was one of those who emigrated, because one of his friends in Pioche, John Manning, stated in a court case to be discussed later, that he met Richard on a ship from New Zealand to British Columbia in about 1860-1862. We know that Australia was the first choice for emigrants leaving County Kerry. Most sailed from the port of Tralee to Liverpool, and then waited in boarding houses near the docks for one to ten days for their designated ship—to Australia. No permits, passports or identification were required to board a ship—if the government of one of the countries had paid for your passage to the ship's Captain, you could go aboard, and that was that!

The general advice from Irish genealogists is to look for records at the various arrival ports to confirm passage. So, based on this advice, I engaged a New Zealand genealogist, Judith Edmonds, who searched vigorously for records pertaining to Richard Moriarty's passage to Australia — to no avail. However, Ms. Edmunds did find one record of a R. Moriarty on a small ship from Victoria, Australia, to New Zealand.

Name: R. Moriarty

Age: 22

Birth year: 1839

Departure Date: Dec. 1861

Destination: Otago, New Zealand

Ship: Atrevida

Ship's Master: Bisset, C. H.

The date of birth is off; however, it was common for
the Irish to use different birth dates at different times
— they were never sure of their date of birth and
often used this to their advantage when needed.
This is certainly not conclusive evidence, but we do
know that Richard did sail from Victoria to Otago,
because John Manning then met him on the ship
from Otago to British Columbia, and the dates of
passage work.

There is no clear proof of what Richard did in
Australia; however, many men from Kerry County did
directly enter the gold fields upon arrival. Also, we
know that Richard moved to New Zealand within a
two-year period, where alluvial gold fields were open
to immigrants. The move then to Vancouver, British
Columbia, where he purchased a mining license,
makes his career path into mining conclusive.

Rounding The Cape Of Good Hope

Gold was found in Australia in 1851; and word of this bonanza travelled the globe in a flash, resulting in a massive movement of people from the British Isles, Europe, China, and America. By 1858, the population in the Victoria gold fields had peaked at 150,000. The Suez Canal was not opened until 1869, so in the late 1850's, the journey from Liverpool to Victoria, Australia, would have taken three to four months on a sailing ship—most likely in steerage. Also, some emigrants, mostly men, were traveling on freighters. Since we don't know exactly when Richard left Ireland or whether his passage was assisted, we can only speculate on the type of ship on which he sailed. However, we do know, other than the newer clipper ships, all the ships sailing from Great Britain to Australia were sailing directly south following the western coast of Africa around the Cape of Good Hope and eastward across the Indian Ocean to Australia. Some ships would veer westward on the way south and dock briefly in Brazil to trade and take on more supplies, but many would make the full journey without stopping.

Travel on the high seas in the mid 1800's was always treacherous. It would be impossible to travel for four months and not encounter a major storm somewhere along the way. And then, there was life to live during the 90-plus days at sea—hard to read about, and even harder to imagine. There were issues with poor hygiene, low ventilation in steerage, no lights, the use of candles or oil lanterns, cramped conditions, timber, or straw mattresses, limited and sometimes poorly cooked food, and illnesses — not to mention the lack of lifeboats, and the fact that few people could swim. Many lives were lost during these journeys on almost every ship. How must this journey have been tolerated for an Irish teenager, possibly traveling alone.

Gold miners of that era are difficult to trace. The early mining was all alluvial, which involved panning and washing dirt in small sluice boxes, so sophisticated mining skills were not needed. As the gold was exhausted in each alluvial plain, the human rush would move on to the next plain, so these miners were never in one spot for long.

Eventually, however, as the alluvial plains were worked, the mine owners started to dig deeper for the gold, creating shaft/underground mining that required skilled workers. The Irish were generally lacking prior mining experience and became the unskilled laborers for these large-scale mining operations. However, they made their mark in other ways in the new developing society in Australia. They carried with them their heritage of dramatic storytelling, dancing, and drinking, providing the camps with entertainment during the long evenings. Gambling could probably also be thrown into that category.

The Irish had been rebelling in one way or another against British rule for centuries, and the recent famine had surely exacerbated those tendencies. Since Australia was a British colony, this feeling of disdain for the British by the Irish miners created an undercurrent of rebelliousness, and the Irish took on the role of rabble rousers in the gold field communities. In 1854, a group of outraged Irishmen provided the leadership for the "Eureka" rebellion against the governmental rules for licensing miners. The rebellion was not entirely successful, but ultimately the government changed the amount they charged the miners from 30 shillings to five shillings per year; and when their fee was paid, they were also registered to vote. The miners had gained representation.

Once the immigrant miners referred to as "diggers" reached the working gold field, they had to adjust to the "goldfield" lifestyle — living in tents with a mattress stuffed with local tree leaves and very simple meals cooked over an open fire. When they were working (six days a week) everyone wore a striped undershirt, a blue or red striped flannel over shirt, cotton trousers, leather belt, and heavy leather boots. After a few paychecks, a digger might invest in a Sunday suit of clothes and take a short trip to the nearby stores for supplies.

In time, a miner might progress to a bark hut. Meals were usually fresh meat, or salted meat and "damper," a bread made with baking powder and flour — yes, only baking powder and flour!

From rural Ireland, where the young men mostly helped farm the small potato plots and feed the pigs or goats, working backbreaking shifts panning for gold must have been an incredible physical and psychological trauma for an Irish teenager.

Australia To New Zealand

The Chinese arrived in Australia in the 1850's and 60's in the thousands. They had difficulty getting hired in the gold fields as miners, but quickly adapted and took over the diggings that were being abandoned by the Europeans. With careful and slow methods, they were always able to extract slight bits of gold after the mines were vacated — enough gold to keep them going.

Most of the Chinese had come from the Canton province, where they had been farming laborers. They were extremely proficient farmers and were able to cultivate remarkably successful gardens raising much-needed produce which had been missing in the miners' diet.

This was a whole new world for the young Irish miners who were used to living in small communities consisting mostly of their relatives. Now Richard Moriarty, still a teenager, was living with men from every continent in the world. Unfortunately, the Chinese were relegated to the lowest rung in the mining community's pecking order; and, as always, they made the best of it.

Gold had been discovered in Australia in 1851, so the mining industry was well established and probably at its peak of production when Richard arrived in about 1858 to 1859. I seriously doubt that he could have arrived earlier due to his age. Gold mining is a hard job requiring mature muscles and good health. It would be very difficult for a boy under the age of 16 to do the job. If he had been born in 1842, he would have been 16 in 1858. If he was the boy who was picked up for "absconding from his master," in December 1858; and if he was sent to Australia at that time, he would have arrived maybe mid-year 1859. I realize that this is a lot of "ifs" but, with lack of records, I can only work with suppositions, hoping that more genealogical information might be uncovered in time.

Unfortunately, the gold from the first Australian gold rush started to run out in 1861, and thousands of miners were making plans to rush to the next bonanza. Therefore, the listing of "R. Moriarty" on the ship to Otago in Dec. 1861, tracks perfectly. Our young miner had to move fast, and alluvial mining was still operational in New Zealand, which was a viable option. However, the gold rush rumor mill was always at work. *The Daily Southern Cross* of Auckland, New Zealand, reported on January 3, 1862, "Exciting news comes from the Cariboo country, where the mines are turning out very rich ore...."

The Otago Witness (New Zealand) on February 8, 1862, notes, "If anybody here had entertained doubts as to the truth told concerning the enormous yields of the mines of our sister colony during the season just past, such doubts would have been entirely dissipated had he stood on the Hudson's Bay Company wharf last evening and saw the Otter come in with 70 passengers from Cariboo."

The rush was on to British Columbia — as was Richard Moriarty, now age 20!

Rush To Fraser River, British Columbia

Richard may have mined for a short while in New Zealand, but his sights were surely set on the next big bonanza, if he could get there fast enough — timing is everything for a gold miner.

The British Columbia gold rush had started in 1858, with thousands of California gold miners sailing from San Francisco up the coast to Vancouver Island, where they travelled by paddleboat up the Columbia River and its tributaries to the gold fields.

On December 28, 1858, Governor James Douglas proclaimed that all the gold mines on the Fraser and Thompson Rivers belonged to the British Crown. Then based on information he had gleaned from the Australian government, he set up a system of charging the miners ten shillings ($5.00 U.S.) for a mining license, with a caveat that anyone removing gold without a license would be prosecuted both criminally and civilly.

British Columbia had been declared a Territory on July 1, 1858, so governmental structure and a rudiment of legal structure were set in place early. However, this structure did not extend to documenting immigration. The immigrants arriving in Vancouver simply walked off the boats onto the docks and strolled into Victoria for food and lodging — there are absolutely no records for this period, except for the mining licenses.

The next challenge was how to locate a mining license for Richard Moriarty. My search took me to the Gold Commissioner of British Columbia, who referred me to the Barkerville Historical Society who has maintained excellent records from the days of the Cariboo gold mining rush. Barkerville was the main town in the Cariboo territory, and the volunteers of the Historical Society were successful in finding the record of Richard Moriarty purchasing a license in Barkerville, May 19, 1863! Voila—I couldn't believe my luck. Now I knew for sure where Richard was in 1863. He was now 21 years old.

The route to Barkerville and the Cariboo goldfields was long and incredibly treacherous. Barkerville is 800 Kilometers (497) miles from Vancouver into the Canadian outback. The miners initially followed river tributaries by paddling canoes and sometimes walking the old Hudson Bay trappers' trails. The last 100 miles from Quesnelle to Barkerville were almost totally impassable. Packers lost hundreds of horses and mules along this stretch. The trails were slick and muddy in places, through deep snow-covered mountains, crossing hazardous rivers and creeks. Eventually the Canadian government realized they had to improve this supply route to ensure success for the mine owners, and they completed a passable road in 1865.

Due to dramatic snowfall in the winters, these mines could only operate from late spring until early fall. During the winter months, the miners crowded into boarding houses in Victoria and just waited for the trails to dry out enough to make the journey back to the Cariboo in the spring. Therefore, Richard's gold license, purchased in May of 1863, was at the beginning of the season. He may not have mined in the Cariboo region for more than the 1863 season, and possibly the 1864 season, as word of gold strikes in the States were reaching the Cariboo. Mining in Idaho must have sounded like a lark after surviving a season in the Cariboo territory of British Columbia.

Although, other than the weather, lack of supplies, living conditions; and the death-defying journey to reach the gold, life at the Cariboo wasn't that bad. On Aug. 17, 1863, the *Cariboo Sentinel* reported on the peacefulness of the creeks, "Everything is very quiet and orderly on the creek owing in great measure to the magistrate, Mr. O'Reilly's efficiency and the wholesome appearance of the Honorable Judge Begbie, who seems to be a terror to evil doers and a sworn enemy to the use of the knife and revolver."

Unlike the California gold districts where the law was vigilante-driven because most of the miners were armed, Cariboo miners were generally unarmed. There were arguments, fights, robberies, and a few murders, but not in the numbers that were occurring in the States. The reason for this can be mostly attributed to the determination of Judge Begbie, who ran a tight courtroom, and used a wide variety of innovative tactics to keep the peace. He was the right man at the right time for maintaining law and order in the wilderness of the Canadian outback.

Once again, just like the Australia gold rush, miners were making their way to Vancouver from all over the globe. "Minorities were the norm during gold rush days…. there were as many accents in Barkerville as there were shovels."[15]

The Chinese were some of the first to arrive with an average sailing time of 60 days. In 1858, 1,669 Chinese left the Guangdong province and were mining on the Fraser River before the end of the summer. By early 1860, more than 1,000 Chinese were working on the Cariboo Road and had opened small shops all along the route. They formed associations with their friends and neighbors call "tongs," and generally felt that they were treated more fairly in Canada than had been their experience in the California gold districts.

This melting pot of humanity provided color and interest to the lives of the miners, but nothing compared to the arrival of women! Some wives followed their husbands, others arrived on "bride-ships," receiving proposals of marriage as soon as they walked onto the docks at Victoria.

"Many, if not most, women who came to the creeks, married there. Often marriage certificates hinted at past lives, while obituaries were edited for refinement and respectability. A former dancehall girl was remembered posthumously as a midwife; a prostitute's past was forgotten."[16]

But then, there were the Hurdy dancers and the prostitutes who hadn't married. "Hurdy Dancers and prostitutes were referred to by their first name or a nickname, if at all. Madams and businesswomen were known by their last name, when mentioned."[17]

Unfortunately, prostitutes have always been a vulnerable population, especially when placed in an environment where they are significantly outnumbered by men. For example, in 1862, Johanna Maguire earned $3,000 in one season at the Williams Creek mining district. Upon leaving, she was ambushed, losing her money and her horse. Then penniless, she moved in with Edward Whitney in Victoria, where he beat her regularly. Johanna died after a vicious beating, but the inquest said that she died of "over-drinking," and Whitney went free. Many like-kind situations occurred with the local prostitutes who are buried in Camerontown or Richfield, British Columbia cemeteries in unmarked and unrecorded graves.

The "Hurdy Gurdy" girls had it quite a bit better—they were dancing girls, originally known as "Terpsichorean artistes," according to the *Sentinel* newspaper. Their name comes from the musical instrument used for their dancing accompaniment. The Hurdy Gurdy is played with buttons like an accordion, but it also has a wheel that rubs against a string, creating a drone which is somewhat like a violin, or maybe more like the tone of a bagpipe. The Hurdy Gurdy and bagpipes were the most popular instruments for dancing in the rural areas of Europe for centuries and were particularly popular in western Germany.

This troupe of Hurdies arrived in Barkerville in 1866. They worked in several saloons for $1 per dance. The girls also got a percentage of the sale of drinks purchased by the miners while in their company. *The*

Sentinel published an interesting letter describing the hurdies in detail:

> "HURDY GURDY DAMSELS. There are three descriptions of the above named "ladies" here, they are unsophisticated maidens of Dutch extraction, from poor but honest parents and morally speaking, they really are not what they are generally put down for. They are generally brought to America by some speculating, conscienceless scoundrel of a being commonly called a 'Boss Hurdy.' This man binds them in his service until he has received about a thousand per cent for his outlay. The girls receive a few lessons in the Terpsichorean art, are put into a kind of uniform, generally consisting of a red waist, cotton print skirt and half mourning headdress resembling somewhat in shape the top knot of a male turkey, this uniform gives them quite a grotesque appearance. Few of them speak English, but they soon pick up a few popular vulgarisms; if you bid one of them good morning your answer will likely be,"itsh sphlaid out" or "you bet your life."
>
> The Hurdy style of dancing differs from all other schools. If you ever saw a ring of bells in motion, you have seen the exact positions these young ladies are put through during their dance. The poor girls as a general thing earn their money very hardly."[18]

Richard Heads South

Since we know for a fact that Richard Moriarty adopted an alias when he arrived in Pioche, it was amusing to find this small ditty in Wright's book on Barkerville. I knew that miners often had nicknames or 'handles" that stuck with them from mine to mine, but I didn't realize that adopting an alias was also common among miners. The song goes as follows:

"What was your name in the States?

Was it Thompson or Johnson or Bates?

Did you run for your life,

Or murder your wife?

Oh, what was your name in the States?"[19]

The Cariboo District was a tough location due to the long winters that made for a short mining season; and the small size of the claims further limited the amount of gold that could be extracted in the three or four-month time. In short, most miners were barely breaking even in the Cariboo district and were forced to look south to the States for new ground — some went to White Pine, Nevada, near Elko, and some to Idaho or Tombstone, Arizona.

Out of these gold mining districts, Richard chose Idaho. Did he know men who had gone there before him? It's a good possibility.

No significant exploration occurred in the Boise Basin until 1862, but when the boom happened it was cataclysmic, and the rush continued through 1866. By 1868, however, the bubble was bursting in the Boise Basin, and miners were again leaving in droves for Montana and Nevada. In fact, thousands of opportunistic miners were, for the better part of the next 100 years, moving around the world globe like a large amoeba — the organism creeping from one hot spot to the next — to the next — to the next, always with the greatest optimism.

The Boise Basin, now home of the city of Boise, Idaho, is in the southwestern part of the state, where the towns of Pioneer City and Idaho City were established in 1862, by the arrival of thousands of men, each carrying a pick and a shovel. The Basin is about 30 miles long and 25 miles wide, and most of its gullies and creeks contained "pay dirt."

William Polock, a miner, reported to the *"Golden Age,"* newspaper February 15, 1862, about his first days on his claim at Granite Creek, in the Boise Basin,

> "We immediately sunk a hole to the bedrock; the prospects were not very flattering until we reached it, and then the first shovelful made our eyes stick out, for the real stuff was there in all its beauty. We panned out three pans full of dirt, and the proceeds were $11.... The gold is generally coarse about the size of a kernel of corn.... I think there is about 2,000 on Granite Creek or near here."[20]

Once again, Richard was on the move with thousands of his fellow miners from Victoria, British Columbia to the Idaho Territory. It must have looked from the air like an infinite chain of ants crawling from

Victoria, through Seattle, probably due south to Portland, and then directly east crossing the Cascade Range for an easy stroll southeast across the Columbia Plateau into the Boise Basin.

How did the miners travel these distances? It is 630 miles from Victoria to Boise. The miners could walk, ride a donkey if they could afford to buy one and feed it, or hitch a ride on a cart or wagon carrying freight; or, if you had done well at the Cariboo, you just might ride a coach via Wells Fargo. In any event, it had to take a month to get to the Boise gold field due to the winter weather, and there had to be quite a few months of down time between these treks from the old gold field to the new one — lots of time to catch up on stories, drink, gamble and practice shooting.

By 1865, Richard had settled in and was mining in the nearby town of Pioneerville, sometimes called Pioneer City, one of four camps in the Boise Basin, boasting a population of 2,743, where the initial type of mining was panning for gold in the creeks and sandbars. However, by 1863, many mine owners were pursuing quartz, which required investors to pay for the expenses of digging and erecting deep shafts. Interestingly, one investor who was drawn to the area was W. H. Raymond, from the Raymond and Ely mine in Pioche; and another, the famous investor, George Hearst, father of Randolph Hearst.

In searching Idaho census records and other genealogical records, I came across a miner named James Moriarty, who had located in Idaho the same time period as Richard Moriarty— could they be related? I have tried to tie these two together in a family tree but have been unable to confirm any kinship. Who knows when someone will come along and put this puzzle together?

I will place the clues that I have on these two Moriarty's side by side and see what you think:

Richard Moriarty	James Moriarty
Born 1842-1843	Born 1837-1838
Cahersiveen, Kerry	Caherdaniel, Kerry
Parents – Unknown	Parents – unknown
Arrives Australia	Arrives Australia
(About 1859)	(Dec. 16, 1859)
Arrives British Columbia	British Columbia
(About 1862 – 1863)	(About 1860 -1862)
Leaves B.C. 1863	Leaves B.C. 1863
Arrives Idaho	Arrives Idaho
(1863 – 1865)	(July 4, 1863)
Fenian Involvement	Fenians
(1865, 1866, 1867)	(1867)
Leaves for Nv 1868	Stays in Idaho

James Moriarty, based on his reported statements in the "*History of Idaho*," left British Columbia in 1863, arriving in Placerville, Idaho July 14th. Were Richard

Moriarty and James Moriarty travelling together, or was Richard following purposely in James' tracks?

The Boise Basin was a "happening" place at that time—lots of gold being extracted, lots of buildings going up, and lots of drinking and gambling in the many bars. In 1863, Richard would have been 21 years old. The Basin was one of the richest gold rushes in the world. It is estimated that between 1862 and 1882, $250 million dollars of gold was extracted. By the middle of September 1863, Idaho City had become the largest city in the northwest, boasting nine restaurants, 25 to 35 saloons, as well as doctors, lawyers, two jewelers, a bowling alley, and a mattress factory. However, this magnitude of gold production paired with a population explosion, made up mostly of men under age 35, culminated in an environment of too much drinking, fighting and too many guns — a bad trifecta!

Law was weak in the Basin. *"The Daily Alta"* reported that during the summer of 1863, "Crime is frequent, homicides occur almost every day. There are no churches or schools." Many miners were carrying pistols on the goldfields in Australia, and some were carrying on the Cariboo in British Columbia. It is probable that a man as young as Richard Moriarty would have needed protection and would most likely have purchased a gun before he arrived in Idaho, or soon thereafter.

Who Are The Fenians?

Richard Moriarty and James Moriarty both joined the Fenian movement in Idaho, which was sometimes referred to as the "Clan na Gael" in the U.S. Our globetrotting gold miners were now involved in Irish politics.

Irish immigrants, accustomed to living near their blood relatives, always stayed close to one another in their new location. They were all vitally interested in what was happening in the old country, some sending money back home on a regular basis. And, they were forever and always angry at the British government, which was a way of life for the Irish with few exceptions.

The Irish had put up with British rule on their God-given homeland since the 1500's, and their view of it was not improving over time. Children were raised knowing from the time they first walked that the British were to be tolerated in public, but secretly despised — your clan first and foremost at all times.

A great surge of grass roots sentiment to, once and for all, throw out the British, arose in the southwest part of Ireland in the 1860's, in County Kerry, to be exact—Richard Moriarty's birthplace. This movement grew into an organization called the 'Fenians;' dedicated to the pursuit of Irish independence from the British, by force if needed, and calling for the complete separation of Church and State. In England, Church and State, even to this day, are not separate, as they are in the U.S. And the Fenians felt that the English Church was, and is, part of the Irish problem.

The Fenians were very much in touch with the Irish in America, and, in fact, needed Irish men who had been soldiers in the Civil War to return to Ireland to fight in a planned uprising. They also needed the American Irish to raise funds to support the movement.

The *"Idaho World"* ran an ad December 20, 1865, for "A Grand Fenian Ball to be given by the Emmet Circle of Fenian Brotherhood at Okanagan Hall, Pioneer City, Monday, Jan. 1, 1866. Serving on the Committee of Arrangement is R. Moriarty, and others." Tickets were sold for $8.

A second Ball was advertised in *"The Idaho World,"* June 16, 1866, to be held at the City Hotel, Idaho City, on the Fourth of July. On the invitation committee for Pioneer City is R. Moriarty and others.

Again, *"The Idaho World"* reports on March 9, 1867, "A Fenian District Convention, which was held March 2nd in Centerville, to choose a District Head — one delegate from Pioneer City is R. Moriarty, and one delegate from Samsfield Circle is J. Moriarty." They may not have been closely related, but they were certainly related, as they were both members of the Moriarty clan of County Kerry, and they were obviously in contact with one another.

In 1867, about 10,000 Fenian Rebels staged a flurry of skirmishes in several locations in Ireland, but they were quickly suppressed by the British army. Only 12 lives were lost, but thousands of Fenians in Ireland were imprisoned.

Chinese Follow The Gold

We have learned from Australia, New Zealand, and British Columbia, that as soon as the gold thins out and the pans and sluice boxes are almost bare, the European miners leave in a bunch, and Chinese miners move in to glean the tailings. When the gold fields of California were picked dry by the mid-1850's, Chinese miners moved north into Oregon, Washington, and British Columbia, and by 1870, close to 30% of the population of Idaho was Chinese.

They had left China for the same reasons others had emigrated from Europe — land shortages for farmers, natural disasters, and war, which for the Chinese was the Taiping Rebellion. As in California, Washington and Oregon, the Chinese were persecuted horribly in Idaho. An economy based on short, unsustainable periods of gold discovery, accompanied by newly created territories with weak government, and topped off with a majority Caucasian population carrying a deep-seated hatred of different races, made for hopelessly cruel treatment of the Chinese immigrants.

The Europeans were learning to tolerate the cultural differences between the citizens of various European countries, but accepting Asians was beyond their tolerance level at that time in history.

On Nov. 23, 1866, *"the Idaho World"* reported: "A KILLING AFFAIR":

"A Chinawoman was shot dead in her own house in Pioneer City last Saturday evening, in a most wanton, wicked barbarous manner. It appears that the wretched creature passed a little knot of men in the street, and in sheer devilishness some of them commenced to shoot at her. The poor thing ran for her life and reached her abode, but there, through the closed door, one fatal shot reached her, and she fell dead. Sheriff Crusher hurried to the place, and he and Deputy Sheriff Gorman separately arrested three men there early in the week, named R. Moriarty, John Manning, and Wm. Miles, who are charged with participation in the shooting. They were examined before Chief Justice McBride and held to answer at the next term of Court in the following amount: Moriarty, $2,500; Manning, $1,000; Miles, $1,000. They each found sureties and were released. The Chinese testimony, upon which they are held, is of the most contradictory and unreliable character. The witness who Tuesday testified so emphatically that Moriarty shot the woman, at the examination of Miles on Thursday evening swore just as positively that he (Miles) shot her."

It appears that the prosecution could not indict these men due to the conflicting testimony of this witness, so all three were released. Oh, the luck of the Irish!

Well, we now know that Richard Moriarty had a pistol and knew how to use it; and that the murder of a Chinese woman in cold blood did not tarnish his reputation in Idaho, as he was an elected delegate to a Fenian convention three months later; and that he and John Manning who had met on the boat from New Zealand to British Columbia had reunited in Idaho, if not before.

As the researcher and author of this book, I cannot emphasize enough how shocked I was when this newspaper article appeared as a result of a routine Google search. I literally became weak at the knees and felt faint. I, of course, had been up to this point romanticizing my chosen character, the swaggering, handsome, very Irish Richard Moriarty, and now my visions were dashed; and how, as the writer do I deal with this alarming information without harming the story?

It took days to process this information and to decide how to proceed with my characterization of Richard, who was turning into such a bad boy. I ultimately concluded that my only choice was to present everything I could find about Richard and let you, the reader, draw your own conclusions. He was obviously born into a terrible social and political mess in Ireland; was forced to separate from his family and emigrate from his sheltered homeland. Also, he had been the victim of considerable denigration by the English while growing up, who thought of the Irish as less than human. Then he was exposed to the Chinese in Australia, where they were treated by the British as even less than human than the Irish. We must take these things into consideration before drawing conclusions. And so, I took a deep breath and moved forward in telling this exciting tale.

Timing Is Everything

Being a miner of precious metals is a tricky business to say the least. You must be physically strong, healthy, able to work long hours six days a week with cold hands, cold feet, in a stream or creek bed in some deep canyon or on a sand bar with swift, moving water on either side. And to sleep in a tent or dug out, surviving on hardtack, a few roasted wild animals, and beans. Or, you can mine underground — the same long hours six days a week, the same tent, or maybe you get lucky and move into a crowded boarding house built on a steep hill on the side of some very remote mountain top. You ride a lift down 400 to 1,000 feet and chip away at rocks by candlelight for ten to 12 hours a day, eating a can of sardines for lunch, sitting on cold ground leaning up against a stope.

However, the rewards are there! You make at least twice as much as other laborers, drivers, butchers, and bakers. You are admired because you can afford good boots, good liquor, and a fancy gun. You can afford to walk with a swagger. You have plenty of money to pick up the tab for your buddies at the saloon, to enter any back room gambling game, to dance and drink with the hurdies, and to top off the evening with a night cap at the local brothel.

Now, all of that is difficult enough to carry off, but this juggling act gets even faster. Precious metals lodged tightly into small pockets of granite or quartz or lying inconspicuously among grains of sand in a creek bed or on a sand bar, are a finite product. Once extracted, they are gone forever —never to return.

All mine fields become barren at some point. And the mining must cease at the very moment when the last nugget is placed on the last car, truck, or railroad car to be carried to the mill. It's over, and so is the paycheck.

A miner must pack up his tools and supplies and make haste to the next active mining field to register for the next payroll; because if he can't do this successfully, the drinking, gambling, hurdy girls, and, of course, the swagger are going to be left behind.

How does a miner know when to leave one mine and head to the next? Do you ride the decline to the bitter end at your current location, or do you hit the road as soon as you see the decline starting to happen, and hurry to the next hot spot before a thousand other miners get the same idea?

When you buy your first pick, shovel and gold pan, there is no crystal ball in the package, so it is a vicious game that miners must play based on a relentless abundance of rumors; some based on facts and some completely baseless, accompanied by one's own intuition.

Let's trace Richard's movement in the total scheme of the world's gold rushes during the 1800's to see how he was doing with this wild game of "rush and seek." Richard was a relative latecomer to the Australian gold rush which had begun in 1851 — he arrived about 1858, inexperienced, and was one of 100,000 miners. He was forced by the declining ore in

Australia to leave for New Zealand, and he might have already set his sights on British Columbia, as rumors of Frasier River gold riches had already reached New Zealand by 1861.

The huge rush to the British Columbia Fraser River began April 25, 1858, when a shipload of California gold rush miners arrived. Richard arrived about 1863, which was early, but was not on the ground floor, and there were other limiting factors which would have impeded his success in this area. Therefore, timing had not been particularly favorable to Richard. He was getting by, but that's about all. No wonder he took off for Idaho, based on new rumors. He was in a position, along with many other miners, that demanded moving to the next hot spot. He was still young and considered unskilled in the mining industry, as most of his experience was alluvial mining — panning for gold. He would not have been able to get much experience in quartz mining up to this point. The placer mining was played out, leaving the need for fewer miners to mine the underground ore (lode miners), so most of the miners were, once again, on the road heading south.

Oysters And Champagne Crowd of Virginia City

Sometime between October 1866 and November 1868, Richard followed the gold to Virginia City, Nevada. It is more than 100 miles between Boise and Virginia City, but there were stagecoaches or freight wagons running frequently between all the gold rush towns. Richard would have travelled west through the southeastern part of Oregon, then straight south to Winnemucca, Nevada, where he could have caught a ride west to Carson City. The Central Pacific railroad was not completed until 1869, but there was a steady stream of wagon traffic across that route — approximately where east/west I-80 runs today.

By 1868, Virginia City was a very desirable place to live, "a real hot spot," especially if you were a young miner looking for a better paying mine and for some fast-paced living. Virginia City was a party town like no other, perched on the side of Mount Davidson, a grand mountain in the Virginia Range, just one beautiful valley east of the Sierra Nevada Mountain range and Lake Tahoe — an unlikely place for a gold rush, but even more unlikely for a town where buildings were built on the side of a 40% grade.

The town is at an elevation of 6,200 feet with a somewhat treacherous road reaching up from the Carson Valley   - one hairpin turn after another. Every piece of mining equipment, lumber for supporting the mine shafts, as well as furniture, food, and clothing, had to be imported from San Francisco, crossing the Sierras, the Carson Valley, and then ascending the high grade into Virginia City.

It's almost incomprehensible as to how this was accomplished, but, in short, the trails across the Sierras had become a solid, single line of wagon traffic from Sacramento to Virginia City, which included gold miners walking to the next gold rush, some with picks and shovels over their back, and the more fortunate leading or riding their burro.

The discoveries of gold and silver on the Comstock were dramatically lucrative, as were the pocketbooks of the mine owners, bankers, investors and trickling on down to the miners. Mark Twain described Virginia City best with the fewest words, "Nothing was on the level, figuratively and literally."[21] The appetites of the residents quickly matched the drama of the discovery, and in no time, the freight wagons were carrying dresses imported from Paris, fine European furniture, pianos, opera singers from San Francisco, fine wine and, can you believe it, oysters! Nothing was too good for, or too inaccessible for the Comstock crowd.

In 1860, the total male population of Virginia City was 2,778, and by 1870 it had exploded to 6,598 — 42% were miners and 58% support workers. There were citizens of more than a dozen different countries — Ireland, Britain, China, Germany, Canada, Mexico, Central and South America, France, Switzerland, Italy, Scandinavia, and Portugal. By 1870, out of a total population of 11,319 — 2,160 were Irish.

Richard Moriarty was not alone in Virginia City. Gold Hill, a small town about a mile downhill from Virginia City had compiled an official city directory, where we first find William Kelly (in years 1868, 1869 and 1871), a cousin of Moriarty's who we will meet again later, and John Manning (in years 1868, 1869), Moriarty's shipmate from New Zealand to British Columbia, and Idaho shooting buddy. James Moriarty had remained in Idaho.

The Irish were the largest immigrant group represented on the Comstock, where they had become a dominant force in the community. They were able to assimilate easily and did not experience the religious prejudices against their Catholic faith, as did their brethren on the Atlantic seaboard.

In 1864, the Irish in Nevada formed a unit of the Emmet Guard, that became a forerunner of the Nevada National Guard. This organization was closely associated with the Fenian Brotherhood which was very active in the Boise Basin mining district and was a precursor to the Irish Republican Army. I'm certain our Irish blokes became members of this group immediately upon reaching Virginia City. In fact, the *"Territorial Enterprise"* printed an ad for The Second Annual Grand Military and Civic Ball to be given at Fort Homestead, Gold Hill on Wednesday Evening, June 10th. Guess who is on the reception committee? Rick Moriarty and William Kelly. Tickets were $3. Oh, how I wish I could have been there!

Included in the various excesses on the Comstock were drinking and gambling. Nevada author and historian, Eliot Lord, in his book, *"The Roar and the Silence,"* gives us a tantalizing view of the Virginia City nightlife:

> "Little stacks of gold and silver fringed the monte tables and glittered beneath the swing lamps. A ceaseless din of boisterous talk, oaths, and laughter spread from the open doors into the streets. The rattle of dice, coin, balls, and spinning-markers, flapping of the greasy cards and chorus of calls and interjections went on day and night, while clouds of tobacco smoke filled the air and blackened the roof-timbers, modifying the stench rising from the stained and greasy floors, soiled clothes, and hot flesh of the unwashed company."[22]

It was reported that Virginia City had 100 saloons. Mark Twain once said, "Vice flourished luxuriantly during the heyday of our flush time. The saloons were overburdened with customers; so were the police courts, the gambling dens, the brothels, and the jails — unfailing signs of high prosperity in a mining region."[23] Richard Moriarty was a good fit for this fast-living Virginia City crowd.

And, once again, our Irish bloke makes the news in *the Gold Hill Dailey News*, November 16, 1868: "More blood! – Another Victim – About half-past ten o/clock Saturday evening John O'Toole, a miner from the Imperial mine, Gold Hill, was shot and most probably mortally wounded by a man named Rick Moriarty, at a saloon on B Street, Virginia, near Niagara Hall."

I read three or four versions of this shooting, and after considerable review of each report, I concluded that the *Pioche Daily Record* of October 3, 1872, was probably the most accurate. The reporter of this article would have had the advantage of taking his information from the original investigative report in Virginia City. The other articles written immediately after the incident would have relied on only the witnesses who would talk to a reporter. *The Pioche Daily* report is as follows:

> "The circumstances of the killing were about as follows: Dan Lyons had given a soiree, and at or after the dance, Moriarty stepped into the barroom in front and called for a glass of port or some other wine. Pat Lyons...was keeping bar and had been drinking some. In passing out the drink called for he made a mistake in the bottle and gave Moriarty whisky instead of wine. The latter made some remarks about the matter, when Lyons told him 'It was good enough for him anyway,' or words too that effect. Moriarty took offense at the remark and made a demonstration as if to strike Lyons, when John O'toole, who was in the act of drinking at the time, drew up his glass and told Moriarty that if he struck Lyons, he, O'Toole, would strike him. The barroom was filled with men at the time, and Moriarty, drawing his pistol and pointing it at the crowd, backed out of the house, and when outside fired through a pane of glass and killed O'Toole. It was understood at the time that Moriarty claimed that O'Toole had thrown the glass at him. The murderer made

his escape and was never heard of as Richard
Moriarty. Morgan Courtney and Richard
Moriarty are one and the same person."

O'Toole was about 25 years old, and reported to be a
quiet working miner, who happened to be at the
dance that evening. Could the two men have known
each other prior to that evening and had a dislike for
one another? It's quite possible that they could have
worked at the same mine in Gold Hill and crossed
paths in one of the many tunnels running under the
town.

I wondered if Richard had fled on foot down the
mountain to Carson City or Dayton and caught a ride
on a freight wagon heading toward eastern Nevada or
back to Idaho. However, the *"Gold Hill Daily News"*
also published each day the names of passengers
arriving and departing via Wells Fargo Coach lines.
Lo and behold, on November 23, 1868, about one
week after the murder of O'Toole, a "Mr. Moriarty"
was listed as a departing passenger from Gold Hill on
a Wells Fargo coach — no destination given.

There were several Moriarty's on the Comstock at
that time, but none had the first name initial of "R,"
so there is a good chance that this passenger was our
Richard. Both John Manning and William Kelly were
listed in the Gold Hill directory in 1868 and could
easily have enabled Richard to hide out in various
cabins, lean-to shacks, or vacant tunnels for a week
prior to catching the stage. We must remember that
it is always, "Clan first," and government is way down
the list from there. It's highly probable that these two
would have helped with his escape. It's also hard to

say how thorough the police investigation would have been. Did the police have the manpower for an all-out search of the two communities — probably not. Oh, the luck of the Irish!

Gunfighter's Training Camp

There is a gap of two years before Richard reappears in Pioche as Morgan Courtney, and these two years have been a mystery. Some historians have reported that Richard told people in Pioche that he had returned to Ireland for several years. However, after uncovering a few more pieces of information, it appears to me that the "returned to Ireland" statement was more than likely a decoy to keep folks from inquiring about him in the neighboring states.

Charles Convis noted in his book, "*Outlaw Tales of Nevada*," "He said he had come from Salt Lake City, although he may have spent some time in Montana after fleeing from Nevada."[24] Timothy O'Brien testified in a court trial in Pioche, "I have known Courtney three or four years. I knew him at Gold Hill in Nevada. We did not come here together. I have not been prospecting with him here. I did not go to Arizona with him or to Idaho, or to Montana." This testimony further supports the theory that Moriarty did not return to Ireland during the years of 1868 to 1870.

Because of this testimony, I searched newspapers in Arizona, Idaho, and Montana for the years November 1868 until September 1870. I had been curious about this two-year period-of-time between Virginia City and Richard's grand entry into Pioche. Where was he, and what was he doing? He was a petulant, compulsive young Irish immigrant in Virginia City, and then he enters Pioche as a hardened, seemingly experienced gunfighter. What happened in the interim? Where did the money come from for the Henry rifle and the expensive suits and boots? I found two very interesting items in the *White Pine News*, that had been picked up from the Idaho papers:

Giddy...up — Haw! (Another left turn)

"The White Pine News," August 20, 1870, reports, "Arrest of Robbers; August 19, 1870: Snake River, August 19' – three men were arrested by Mr. Davis, near Rose Fork. They were arrested first for horse stealing and then suspicion pointed to them as being concerned in robbing the coach. Their names are Courtney and Kirby."

Again, *The White Pine News*, "Aug. 30, 1870: Malad City, Aug. 29: Courtney and Burns broke jail here last night and escaped. They were in on a charge of horse stealing, and implication in recent coach robberies." Richard had obviously adopted an alias shortly after fleeing from Virginia City, and now he was committing more crimes under a new name, Morgan Courtney.

Rose Fork, Idaho, is on the Snake River, in an area that is now a large reservoir close to Pocatello, Idaho; and Malad, where the arrest took place, is directly south of Pocatello about 13 miles north of the boarder with Utah — a straight shot south to Salt Lake City, and familiar territory for Moriarty, aka Courtney, from his mining days in Pioneer City. Could Morgan Courtney have outfitted himself with a new fancy suit, boots, and possibly a new Henry rifle in Salt Lake City, bought a ticket for a Wells Fargo coach seat to Pioche, Nevada, all purchased from proceeds of a stagecoach robbery; and then arrived there to start his new career, or to further a career that had blossomed during the past two years — a professional gunfighter?

I've wondered why he picked the name, Morgan Courtney. There were a number of Courtney or Courtenae families in County Kerry, Ireland, and I suspect that he was related to one of these families. It seems like the new Morgan Courtney, robber, and killer, knows that from this point on, he must live by the gun, and he has prepared himself to do so.

After rereading a few of the proof sources regarding this period, I serendipitously ran across a quote that I had previously overlooked. It hadn't meant anything to me before. Leo Schafer, *"Boot Hill – The Pioche Cemetery"* had quoted author Neill C. Wilson, who had written, *"Silver Stampede – The Career of Death Valley's Hell-Camp, Old Panamint,"* written in 1937:

> "Tom Kirby, who had been herding with the Morgan Courtney gang…had become a professional strong-arm whom mine owners over a wide territory hired to come and clean up labor and claim-jumping conditions. He maintained his own wrecking crew of toughs and it was said that his unwrapped rifles and revolvers, bearing his name neatly engraved, when shipped into a town by Wells Fargo were usually enough to quell any disorder, whether or not their owner followed in person."[25]

This quote is slightly ambiguous as to who was the leader of the gang, Kirby or Courtney, but after locating Wilson's book and reading the original quote, I believe that he meant that Courtney was the Chief and Kirby a member of the gang. Wilson writes as follows: "Up the canyon from the west came also small Tom Kirby, who had been herding with the Morgan Courtney gang at Fish Springs, a hundred and fifty miles northward. Morgan Courtney, Kirby's old chief, following the Washington and Creole battle at Pioche....[26]

It then became apparent that Courtney must have been jailed with Kirby in Idaho after the horse stealing event and possible stagecoach robbery. The two-year unexplained period started to shape up in my mind. Did Richard Moriarty flee Virginia City after the coldblooded killing of an innocent man in a bar, and change his name to Morgan Courtney? Did he then spend the next couple of years running with a bad gang of criminal rebels, rising to the top of the pecking order, while honing his skills with weapons and with plots involving the element of surprise and threatened violence— like stagecoach robberies?

Wilson places Courtney as the chief of the rebels, and the boss man who had his guns shipped into the subject towns by Wells Fargo — what a tactic to draw interest and perhaps some fear into the local townspeople — a theatrical device right out of Hollywood. Morgan Courtney never lacked imagination or bravado!

Author, Leo Schaffer also quotes Charles Gracey, "On his arrival he handed three hotel checks to the clerk and asked him to have his baggage sent from Salt Lake. When the baggage came it proved to be a small satchel, a Henry rifle, and a six-shooter, each article bearing the name of Morgan Courtney." [27]

I now knew where Richard Moriarty aka. Morgan Courtney had been, what he had been doing, and who he now was. The rest of the story is Morgan Courtney living out his own self-constructed legend.

Saloon Banter Leads To Violence

Giddy... up — Gee!

And now, we are back to where we started with Courtney living the high life in Pioche after raking in $15,000 from the Raymond and Ely mine caper.

On June 8, 1872, a group of Pioche men were playing cards in the back room of Clancy's Saloon: John Wilson, John Baker, and Morgan Courtney. They were playing for drinks. However, Courtney had recently sworn off hard liquor and was drinking sarsaparilla, (original name for root beer.)

After playing for a few hours, the trio moved into the saloon area and were standing at the rear of the bar, when entered James Sullivan, Mr. Murphy, and Mr. Conners. Sullivan then saunters over to Courtney and asks him to have a drink with him. Courtney declines saying that he is already drinking with friends. Sullivan aggressively asks Courtney a second time to drink with him and Courtney declines and says, "let it go at that." Courtney and friends walk out of the bar and are standing directly outside the door on Main Street. Sullivan and company follow, with Sullivan again approaching Courtney, and asking Courtney to go somewhere with him. Courtney said he didn't understand. Sullivan says he wants to give Courtney 62 ½ feet, in the American Flag mine, meaning a share of the value. At that time using feet was the common measurement of "shares" in a mine.

Courtney says he didn't want it. Sullivan says, per Courtney's testimony, "If you don't take it, you're a damned dirty son of a bitch. I asked him if he meant what he said by calling me a dirty son of a bitch. He said, you are a damned son of a bitch, and I'll kill you, at the same time putting his right hand on the handle of his knife and his left hand under his right. I jumped back several paces or feet, and said, as I was going back, 'take that back.' At the same time going after my pistol. As I got my pistol out, I stopped going back. He said as I stopped, or before I stopped, 'I take nothing back, you are a dirty son of a bitch, and I can whip you, or lick you.' From the time that I jumped back till the pistol shot went off, he was following me, not in a direct line... Judge Knight came up and caught me by the collar of my coat and told me I was arrested. I came to jail with him."[28]

Now Courtney is in the Pioche jail, and Sullivan is dead by one shot from Courtney's six-shooter. Courtney was not released on bail and had to spend the entire summer in jail. Attorneys W.W. Bishop and Jesse S. Judge Pitzer were retained for the defense, and Judge Fuller presided over the trial beginning September 13 ,1872. This is the manuscript from the trial that I was able to procure from the basement of the Pioche courthouse. The trial is chock full of information about the style of speech of the times and prevailing customs and attitudes.

First off, the witness list for the prosecution contains 24 names — these are all eyewitnesses to the shooting or to conversation right before or after. The Defense had about the same number. That means that close to 50 people were on Main Street or inside of one of the businesses at approximately 6:00 P.M. on June 8th. The position of the witnesses at the time of the shooting reads something like this:

Horace Beane — Standing at Mr. Folies fruit stand.

P.H. Wand — Standing on corner of Main and Meadow Valley streets with Schoonmaker.

John Conners — Standing 4 to 6 feet from Courtney and Sullivan on sidewalk.

Patrick Murphy — Standing about 10 to 15 feet from the shooting on sidewalk.

William Huntley — Standing in front of Parson's Saloon.

H. Bergstein — Standing Inside Beane's Drug store.

S. Morgan — Standing in door of the telegraph office — 50 feet up the street and across from Clancy's.

A.J. Kent — Standing on the 2nd story of White's Building in Dr. Nicholson's office.

Henry Rives — Standing in front of Felsenthal's, below Clancy's Saloon.

Most of the witnesses testified to seeing the event play out very closely to the way Courtney reported it — some variations as to the location of Sullivan's knife, whether he was carrying any other weapons, the exact position of Courtney's arms at various points, and the position of Sullivan's hands and arms. M. W. Fox testified: "When Sullivan was carried to the rear of Jesse Bean's drug store, I examined the body.

He was partially dead at this time. I believe I took a knife from his person. The knife was on the left side of Sullivan inside his pantaloons. It was in the sheath, somewhere about the guard."[29]

Therefore, Courtney shot a man who was carrying a knife — not a gun — and who had not pulled the knife out of the sheath. Courtney was being challenged by Sullivan, for sure, and being an experienced gunman, Courtney saw his shot and did not hesitate to take it.

Bat Masterson wrote in "*Famous Gunfighters of the Western Frontier*, "Any man who does not possess courage, proficiency in the use of firearms, and deliberation had better make up his mind at the beginning to settle his personal differences in some other manner than by an appeal to the pistol."[30]

One of the more interesting discoveries in the trial for me was the fact that Courtney testified on his own behalf, and so his voice carries from 1872 into the present in 29 handwritten pages of testimony.

I had previously wondered if Gaelic may have been Courtney's first language and English his second. Courtney, raised speaking Gaelic, had become a polished and erudite English speaker as demonstrated in this question/answer volley with the prosecuting attorney:

Question: "Was not the first remark of Sullivan, 'Courtney, did you take a drink?'"[31]

Answer: "He made use of some of the words, but not all of them. He did not use the word 'did' nor the word 'you.' He said, 'Courtney take a drink.' Those are the exact words, as near as I can recollect."

Oh my, this Irishman could dissect a sentence faster than he could fire a six-shooter. And again:

Question: "Why were not Tim O'Brian and Manning called on your behalf as witnesses before the magistrate?"

Answer: "I didn't think you have any right to ask that question; however, I'll answer it."

And now our Irishman is a legal scholar, as well?

The upshot of Courtney's testimony was that he had been warned by several people that Sullivan was out to kill him, and that Sullivan had called him a "son of a bitch" several times and that he would not take it back. Also, he said, and several witnesses testified that Sullivan also said something to the effect that "I can lick you, or I can whip you." It's hard for us to understand this level of violence over being called a name, because even though calling someone an S.O.B. is not a very nice thing to do, and might start a fist fight, those are not words that usually provoke further violence in our society today. However, in the 1800's, this was just not the case. This epithet was simply unforgiveable — it attacked your character, your mother's character, and actually the character of your entire bloodline, and it could not be tolerated in any way, any time, or any place. Calling Courtney a killer would probably not provoke him to pull his six-shooter, but calling him a "son of a bitch," was the end of the line. If the other man was willing to retract his words, their differences could continue to be negotiated, but when Sullivan would not retract his statement, Courtney had to defend the honor of his family, and that was that.

Sullivan Challenges Courtney On

Main Street

Courtney jumped backwards several steps after he heard those words to gain distance from Sullivan. He thought Sullivan was going for a weapon, so he took the shot with his Colt Army revolver. All six chambers were loaded. The first shot was accurate, and Sullivan went down.

We know Morgan Courtney quite well by this time, but who was Sullivan, and what was driving him? All that I could find about James Sullivan was from testimony at the trial, so I will try to summarize with excerpts, so that the exact language of the witnesses can be absorbed.

John Conners – Witness for the Prosecution: "I had eight or ten drinks at the theatre or Opera House (a bar.) I was there at 10 o'clock in the morning till about half past four in the afternoon. I believe I went directly from the Opera House to Clancy's Saloon.... I saw a knife upon the person of Mr. Sullivan that day. I first saw it at the Opera House.... I believe Mr. Sullivan drank with me every time I drank at the Opera House. I was as much under the influence of liquor as James Sullivan – I think not more so."[32]

Charles Peasly – Witness for the Defense – "I am a painter and paper hanger whenever I can get any of it to do. I knew the deceased, James Sullivan, in his life time. I was pretty well acquainted with him for the last year and a half. I met him round several times in saloons and we generally took a drink together. Nothing more than in friendly terms that way. I was in Schulz's hurdy house several times. I was there very often in the month of March last. I couldn't say whether it was in the month of March or not that I was in there with Sullivan. Sullivan and I went to [sic] and after taking a drink there we went to the hurdy house — just as we faced the bar to take a drink, Courtney was going out of the house. Sullivan asked Courtney to take a drink. Courtney says no, I don't want any drink, and walked on out of the house. Sullivan says, the damned 'son of a bitch,' I'll fix him before he gets out of here."

Thomas H. Daley – Witness for the defense (recalled): "I knew Morgan Courtney. I was always on good terms with him, friendly.... We were sitting in Clancy's saloon one night, Peasly and I, talking about some ground. Some wild cat ground I had out here, I'd located once. Peasley, asked if I was friendly with Morgan Courtney — I told him I was. Says he, if he's a friend of yours, I'm not acquainted with him. Tell him to look out for Sullivan, for he swears he'll kill him. I asked him, says I, do you know what's the matter between them? He said something had happened in the hurdy house, some time before; he didn't state what time. I went next morning and told Mr. Courtney every word of it. I think it was between Clancy's and Mr. or Mrs. Wand's opposite the fruit store. That's all I told Mr. Courtney."

Morgan Courtney: The Defendant: "I know that there is such a mining company here as the American Flag. I know the mine. It is an unincorporated company — I [sic] it be so from seeing its stock on the stock board, and it had been unincorporated for a long time before Sullivan offered me the feet in it."

Eugene Ferguson: Witness for the defense: "I reside in Pioche…. I work sometimes. My business is storekeeping. Well yes, I knew the deceased, James Sullivan in Eberhardt White Pine. I also knew him here. Well, no, I knew the man over in White Pine. I had heard his character discussed among parties who knew him. From such discussions among those parties, in reference to his character, his reputation was that of a man violent in his conduct. I know that he carried arms. I have seen them on him myself several times. The last time I saw him, I couldn't say whether it was a large knife or a dagger. I have often seen a pistol on him. I believe it would be a Colt Revolver."

Thomas Daley – Recalled by Defense: "Between 1st and 2nd of May last, Peasley told me what Sullivan had said about Courtney. Courtney and I are good friends. When he first came over here, he slept with me two or three weeks at my room at Mrs. Ryan's house. Mr. Ryan, of the jury, I suppose was there. I was there a month and didn't lay eyes on him." (Yes, beds were scarce in mining camps, and bed-sharing was not looked down upon at that time.)

John Craig – Witness for the Defense: "I have lived in Pioche about two years. I knew the deceased James Sullivan in his lifetime. I knew him by sight…Yes, I knew his character for peacefulness or violence or otherwise, pretty well. His character was not good for peacefulness. His character was bad. I can't say that

I ever heard anything particularly about the man's carrying arms."

Thomas F. Hanley – Witness for the Defense: "I reside in Pioche. I am a saloon keeper. I knew Sullivan in his lifetime. At and about the time of his decease, I knew his reputation for peace and quietness. Was that of a turbulent disposition. By turbulent disposition, I mean that he had both good and bad qualities, and that the bad for the better of the good…Prior to his death he had carried arms. The arms that I saw with him was a six shooter, cut short — sawed off."

There is some interesting commentary from witnesses about Sullivan's comings and goings on June 8th, prior to the shooting. The Prosecution and the Defense were interested in Sullivan's mental state — exactly how drunk was Sullivan, and where had he been that day, and what was he doing? Towards the last days of the trial, several witnesses were found who had some interesting insight to Sullivan's activities on June 8th:

"Testimony in rebuttal for the Prosecution and Defense"

Testimony for the Prosecution:

 H. Tooney: "I was in Pioche on the 8th of June last, the day that Sullivan was killed."

Question: "What was your occupation at that time."

Answer: "I was a butcher."

Question: "Where were you in the habit of sleeping at that time?"

Answer: "In the rear of the market—the People's Market in Meadow Valley Street in the town of Pioche."

Question: "Did you see James Sullivan on the day of his killing."

Answer: "I did".

Question: "When did you first see him in that day and where?"

Answer:" At nine o'clock in the morning, in the People's Market...."

Question: "What became of him then?"

Answer: "He went into my room to sleep."

Question: "Where was that room?"

Answer: "In the rear of the market about 24 feet from the entrance."

Question: "How long did he remain in that room?"

Answer: "Until 2 o'clock..."

Question: "Did you see Sullivan at any time between the time he laid down on the bed, and came out and asked that question?"

Answer: "I did......"

Question: "How did you happen to see him between those times.?"

Answer: "I had to go from the front of the market to the rear several times and saw him there. I passed through from eight to a dozen times just as business

would call me in there..... My room was in the rear of
the market in the same building that I worked in. I
was working for another party, Mr. O'Neil. I did not
tell this to Mr. O'Neil, not that I remember of. I did
not tell it because Mr. O'Neil was passing through the
market himself, and I thought he might have seen it.
Sullivan was subject to sleeping in there. I carried on
my business in the shop. My business is selling and
cutting meats. I am kept pretty busy. ..... I don't
remember how many persons went through there that
day. Mr. Sullivan was subject to sleeping in my room
when he was working out of town and slept in town.
He was in the habit of coming in and throwing
himself on my bed when he was drunk. For eight or
ten days before his death. I was not a particular
friend of Mr. Sullivans, just a passing acquaintance.
This trial does not interest me in the least. I am
perfectly indifferent to it."

Michael Cody:

Question: "Do you remember the day of Sullivan's
death?"

Answer: "I do."

Question: "Did you see Sullivan on that day before
his death?"
Answer: "I did."

Question: "Where did you see him first on that day?"

Answer: "I saw him first in the rear of O'Neal's
butcher shop."

Question: "What was he doing?"

Answer: "He was sleeping."

Question: "On what?"

Answer: "A bed." ...." I went in there about ten o'clock maybe a little after.... I was not in the habit of going through the shop but would sit down in it frequently every day...I had no business there...I came in with my dog. I think Mr. Sullivan was laying on his side on the bed. His feet hung out over the edge of the bed. When I stooped down to tie up the dog. I touched him. I didn't see him at first. I asked, who is this? Someone in the shop [sic] answer, that's Sullivan, don't wake him up."

John Henry: "I knew Mr. Sullivan in his lifetime on the day he was killed. I was butchering for O'Neil and Armstrong. They have two shops one on Main Street and one on Meadow Valley Street. I do the killing, dressing the cattle and delivering the meat in the morning. It takes two of us to do the killing Lewis More and myself.... I was standing by the door in the rear of the shop when he came back, he says it's two o'clock — it's time to go down to the slaughterhouse. We usually went to the slaughterhouse to work about one o'clock. Sullivan was laying on the bed. His shoes lay right at the foot of the bunk."

Cross examination: "Louis Moore was stuffing Bologna sausages in the back room when I saw Sullivan there. There was [sic] and fat in the back room. I had to go through the room to meet Louis Moore and saw Sullivan lying in the bed. I did not see a big [sic] dog there...There was no other dog there.... The bunk was about eleven feet from the front door of the back room. The back room was twelve feet long and 16 feet and three inches wide…. I said it was two o'clock or a few moments after, and I said to Louis it was time for us to be going. He (Sullivan) raised up setting in his bed when Louis and I started to go — but he didn't get off the bed while we were there."

Louis Moore: "I was making sausages on the day that Sullivan was killed — in the room where he was sleeping. The first time I saw James Sullivan in that day was between nine and ten o'clock in the morning. I saw him in the [sic] room where I made the sausage — laying on the bed — right in the rear of the butcher's shop. It is O'Neil's butcher shop…I was making sausage. Mr. Sullivan came in while I was making the sausage. He came in and laid down on the bed…. I guess he went to sleep …I remained there making sausage till about two o'clock in the afternoon. Mr. Sullivan during all this time was laying on the bed. When I went out to the slaughterhouse to kill, I looked at the clock at Gerow's and saw it was two minutes before, or two or three minutes past two o'clock. There was no dog in the room that I know of — not to my knowledge."

Thomas Donahue: "I knew James Sullivan the deceased by sight. I saw him on that day, the 8th of June on Meadow Valley Street in front of the meat market. I think it was between eleven and twelve o'clock that I saw Mr. Sullivan. I and two others were going into Gerow's Saloon. I see one of the men he was talking to in here. I think it was Conner."

Kennedy J. Hanly: "I have stated that I knew James Sullivan the deceased in his lifetime. I saw him on the 8th June last past, on Meadow Valley Street — I should judge a little after eleven o'clock. I seen him crossing the street from the Theatre Saloon towards Gerow's saloon going down the street. I think a gentleman by the name of Mr. Conners and another one I think his name was Murphy was with him."

There we have it — the case of, "Where was James Sullivan on the 8th of June, 1872?"[33] Was he sleeping all morning and early afternoon in the butcher shop with sausage fixings all around him, or was he wandering from saloon to saloon from eleven in the morning until late afternoon when he comes in contact with Courtney in Clancy's saloon? Either way, I think it was fairly clear that by the time he and Courtney squared off, that Sullivan was at the very least somewhat inebriated, and he was surely not thinking clearly, as he brought a knife to a gun fight — a fight that he instigated and had planned to win. Courtney had a six-shooter fully loaded and was drinking sarsaparilla — it was no match.

Alvah C. Bishop, a physician and surgeon, was called to Beene's Drug Store on Meadow Valley Street to examine Sullivan's body. "I saw the body lying there apparently dead — I stooped down and felt his pulse. I considered him dead. He must have died quite recently as the body was quite warm. I examined his body and I saw what appeared to be a gun-shot wound. The wound entered the breast a little to the left of the sternum — to the left of the center of the breast: over the left ventricle of the heart...It seemed to me to have penetrated the body, as near as I could tell by the upper area of it. It looked like a gun-shot wound. If the bullet had continued in a direct line, it would have passed through the heart. If it did go in that direction, the effect as a general thing would have been death in a few minutes....my opinion, as a physician, is that wound was the cause of his death."[34]

Who Knew Morgan Courtney, And When Did They Know Him?

There were three witnesses during this trial who stated they had known Morgan Courtney before knowing him in Pioche. We know the name "Morgan Courtney" was an alias for Richard Moriarty; that Richard was using his real name in Virginia City in 1868; and that he undoubtedly was still on the "Wanted" list in Virginia City for the murder of O'Toole. Since the State of Nevada's prosecuting attorneys in Pioche filed charges using the name Morgan Courtney; it is clear they did not know the real name of their defendant, or that he was wanted in Virginia City. But how about the three witnesses who had known Morgan before — what did they know about him, and when did they know it? Let's examine their testimony in the context of their relationship to Courtney:

John Wilson — was part of the threesome card players in the back room of Clancy's prior to the killing of Sullivan. "I have known Morgan Courtney ever since he has been in this town. I knew him by sight when he was mining in Idaho. I have known him about a year and a half. We were good friends and associates when we met in saloons and on the street. I have been his warm friend since the affair of the shooting and have befriended him. I regard myself as his true, warm friend in this emergency."[35]

(Wilson must have known Courtney as Richard Moriarty in Idaho. He had to know that Courtney was using an alias for some reason.)

<u>Timothy O'Brien</u> — "I reside in Pioche; I am a miner. I was in Pioche on the 8th June 1872. I knew Mr. Courtney. I had seen James Sullivan, the deceased. I saw him on the day in question. I was talking to a friend of mine, Mr. Manning, on Meadow Valley Street I heard Sullivan say there goes Courtney, the 'son of a bitch', and I'll kill him before night.... I have known Courtney three or four years. I knew him at Gold Hill in Nevada. We did not come here together. I have not been prospecting with him here. I did not go to Arizona with him, not to Idaho — nor to Montana."

With this testimony, we know that between Virginia City and Pioche, Courtney was in Arizona, Idaho, and Montana during the two-year period before he entered Pioche. We also know that Timothy O'Brien knew Courtney in Virginia City as Richard Moriarty, and that he could easily have aided Courtney in evading the local police after the shooting of O'Toole. Additionally, O'Brien admits to visiting Moriarty in his cell while he was in jail awaiting this trial. The prosecution alludes several times in their questioning that O'Brien and Manning may have built up Courtney's defense by insisting that Sullivan had spread the rumors that he was going to kill Courtney since the hurdy house incident. This is theory only. But "Clan first and foremost!"

<u>Question to Courtney</u>: "When did you first know John Manning?"

Answer: "About 5 years ago. I should think, probably more. It might have been six."

Question: "Where did you know him?"

Answer: "In Idaho at Pioneer City."

Question to John Manning: "Were you a partner in any matter with Courtney in Idaho?"

Answer: "We were interested together in a mine about a year in Idaho."

Question: "Where were you working on the 8th June?"

Answer: "I was idle for two or three days. I think on the 7th or 6th. The 6th, I believe I got rough sinking a shaft on Panaca flat — the Lightner Shaft I believe — about 100 yards from the main shaft of the Raymond and Ely."

Question: "Who employed you to do this work?"
Answer: "Morgan Courtney."

Later, on cross examination, Manning testifies, "I have known Mr. Courtney over ten years. I knew him in British Columbia — I knew before that on board of a ship. I came in the ship to this country with him from New Zealand. That was 10 years ago. I came to Vancouver Island with him at that time. I knew him there about two years. I was never a partner of his at that time there — I guess about four or five years after I saw him in Idaho. I was not a partner of his there. I wasn't more than a month in Idaho when he left. I think the next time I saw him was at Pioche. I saw him for one day at White Pine. I did not know Mr. Courtney in Australia."

Several days prior, Manning testified, "I have known Mr. Courtney five or six years. I knew him in Idaho. Courtney and I are friends."

Manning admits that he actually crossed by ship from New Zealand to British Columbia with Courtney, so he absolutely knew that he was Richard Moriarty. He says he was in Idaho with him, but, of course, does not say that they both were shooting at a Chinese woman and one of the shots killed her. He neglects to say that they knew each other in Virginia City, and that he probably aided and abetted Richard Moriarty to escape the police after he shot O'Toole.

In other words, the legal system in Pioche arraigned and tried a man who was using an alias, and there were at least two witnesses to the crime who knew that the man being tried was using an alias, and they never blew his cover. "Clan, first and foremost."

After a 12-day trial with the District Attorney's summation lasting five hours, a jury of twelve Pioche residents voted to acquit Courtney. A San Francisco newspaper reported the shooting and the trial this way:

> "The better citizens of this place are about to form a vigilance committee, to rid the country of the many cutthroats and gamblers, who make life risky by their lawless acts. The trouble arises in part by the practice of large mining companies, such as The Raymond and Ely, who hire by the year regular fighters to keep their property. But the worst is that they are often employed to take property, and in undertaking they never hesitate to put out of

the way any man who is an obstacle to their designs. Only the other day a bully named Courtney killed the foreman of the Meadow Valley and is now in jail to answer for a cold blooded a murder as was ever committed. But which employs him, will get him free."[36]

There appear to be other motivations for some of the testimony that were not completely clear from reading the trial transcript. The townspeople noted that the "saloon crowd" pulled hard for Courtney, and that possibly some defense witnesses were not totally on the up and up.

The Luck Of The Irish!

After sitting in the Pioche jail from June 8th to Sept 19th, 1872, Courtney must have breathed a huge sigh of relief when Judge Fuller read the verdict of "Acquittal." He had been detained in the old jail behind the Million Dollar Courthouse —a stone building dug into the side of a Pioche hill — stone walls between the cells — rough cut wood logs and steel bars across the opening to a small room where the jailer sat while on duty — one small window about one foot square in each cell. I can't help but smile when I think of a stone jail in a town filled with miners! Several prisoners were known to have chiseled their way out.

How must Courtney have felt when Virginia City Sheriff Kane came calling, handcuffs in hand, and arrested him for the murder of O'Toole four years earlier? Due to the recent installation of the telegraph, the Sheriffs in each town now had the technology to publicize their outstanding warrants to other jurisdictions. The outcry of townspeople against Courtney required that Sheriff Kane whisk Courtney out of town within hours of the acquittal, as a vigilante committee appeared to be in the works. I'm sure Courtney welcomed a stagecoach ride after 103 days in jail, but not handcuffed to Sheriff Kane for over 400 miles.

Giddy...up — Haw! Hang on — another sharp left turn!

Courtney is back in court in Virginia City, and the District Attorney is forced to file a motion of "*nolle Prosequi*," which means, not proceeding. The bar tender had died, and the remaining witnesses were either dead or, like tumbleweeds, had scattered with the Nevada winds.

Courtney was released — a free man. Oh' The luck of the Irish!

Morgan Courtney Gains A Fresh Start

Now, considering all that had happened in Pioche, one would think that a cagey character like Courtney would take off for some other mining town in Arizona, Colorado, Utah, or back to Idaho. But he didn't; he returned directly to Pioche, knowing that a vigilante committee might be there to greet him. That seems like a big risk, but he had a cadre of very close friends and must have felt he had enough protection. Amazingly, Pioche was a town where infractions could be quickly forgotten — life moved fast in Pioche! Most of Sullivan's friends had already let go of hard feelings, so for the first time in four years, Courtney had no legal repercussions hanging over his head, and he had a new lease on life.

He staked out a new claim for a mine called "The Faro Bank" and teamed up in 1873 with several partners to develop another mine. Courtney also landed a regular job as superintendent of the Kentucky mine in Pioche. It looked like our Irish vagabond was starting to grow roots in Pioche. He joined the "Hook and Ladder" club, and it was rumored that he helped raise funds for the building of the Episcopal church, even though he was Catholic.

He also began a steady Pioche-style relationship with a local woman — Georgianne (Georgie) Scyphers, who was working at a local brothel. Georgie may also have been part of the motivation for Courtney to return to Pioche. She was a woman with spunk and fire. It was reported that once when assaulted by a patron, she shot him with her own pistol. She had also killed a man for defaming her sister — so the story goes. Morgan Courtney had paired up with a woman who was his mirror image. A salty, impulsive, gun-totin' woman for a salty, impulsive, gun-totin' man.

Georgie was also seeing another regular customer, George McKinney. Charles Gracey reported that when one of his millmen told him that a young man from Elko had remarked that he knew Gracey, Gracey inquired "was it the young night watchman from Elko?" When his millman confirmed this, Gracey said, "Mr. Courtney will not be 'Chief' anymore, for this man does not live long in a town that has 'Chiefs.'"[37]

Gracey had remembered McKinney from his time in Elko, Nevada, where McKinney had been working as a night watchman. McKinney had gotten into a contentious card game with a few local timbermen. The next night an angry crowd of woodchoppers descended upon the mill that McKinney was guarding, intending to get even. McKinney was alone and at a huge disadvantage. He handled the angry mob by coming out of the building with two pistols fully loaded and both blazing directly into the midst of the crowd. He killed three men and wounded several others. Not one woodchopper would come forward as a witness, so no charges were filed against McKinney, and his reputation as a gunfighter soared.

There undoubtedly would have been a showdown at some point between Courtney and McKinney, but the small embers burst into flames earlier rather than later, when the two men became enamored with the same "fallen angel," Georgie Scyphers.

Enter: The Girl

It was rumored around town, that the two men had become aware that they were both suitors of Georgie and they started to "square off". On the 31st of July 1873, Georgie had seen McKinney in the morning and had promised to go to his room that night, but she did not show up. The next day McKinney saw her and asked why she had not kept the appointment, and she replied that it was because she was afraid of Courtney. They had agreed to meet in McKinney's room because he was ill. He had not left his room for days — he had been diagnosed by Dr. Lee with a "serious congestion of the bowels, attended by a bilious colic," as per *the Pioche Daily Record*, September 18, 1873.

The next day Aug. 1st, several witnesses testified that they overheard Courtney at around 6:00 p.m. confronting McKinney in front of the Harrison's furniture store saying to McKinney, "You d...n....of a b.... are you here yet? Didn't I tell you to leave town? Now, God d....you, I want you to pay attention to what I say." *Pioche Record*, September 19, 1873.

According to McKinney, Courtney had also threatened him at his room the night of July 30, or early morning July 31, "Courtney was on the ground underneath the window of my room in the Marysville lodging house. I was lying on the bed with my head out the window, in room No.10.... I was very sick and had been confined to my room for a couple of

137

days — had been sick for quite a while..." McKinney further testified that Courtney first said, 'Where is Georgie Scyphers? I remarked that I wasn't keeping cases for Georgie Scyphers.' He said, 'McKinney, you're a d...d cowardly s...of a b…...and if I had hold of you now, I'd make you....'" I said, 'What do you come here to abuse me fore?' He said, 'I'll not only abuse you, but I'll kill you, you d…..d cowardly s...of a b...if you ever cross my path or come in my road. You take my advice and leave town, or I'll shoot the top of your d...d cowardly head off."
Pioche Daily Record, September 18, 1873.

The two coursing planets collided on Aug. 1st, 1873, about 6:00 P.M. in the middle of Main Street in front of Lee's Drug Store. McKinney recounts the encounter this way, "When I first saw Courtney, he was coming towards me very fast; had his hand in his right pocket. I saw him move his hand. I pulled my pistol and fired, saying at the instant of the firing, 'I am here, ready for you.' He stepped on down the street, still facing me, raising his hand out of his coat pocket, when I fired again. He turned clear around and started to run, when I fired again. He ran into the door—the main street entrance of Pres. Wand's saloon — and I followed him as close as I could, and inside the saloon I shot him again — or shot at him — not positive what balls hit him. He ran on out of the Meadow Valley Street entrance with his hand thrown under his coat, like this (as if to draw a pistol). As he got out on Meadow Valley Street I fired again. I followed him a few steps into the street and fired again. He was running from me very fast. I was arrested then and taken away." *Pioche Dailey Record*, September 18, 1873.

The attorney questioned why McKinney had continued to keep shooting after the first shot. McKinney answered the question, "I knew that as quick as I quit shooting that if I hadn't killed him, he'd kill me, knowing the character of the man; that he would not hesitate a moment, if I wasn't shooting at him, to kill me." *Pioche Dailey Record*, September 18, 1973.

The shooting by McKinney was done with a Whistlers patent English pistol. Every chamber of Courtney's pistol was fully loaded. It appeared that Courtney's gun had gotten caught in the pocket of his coat, and he was forced to start running. Unlike the Hollywood version of gun fights, the low-slung holsters were not used in the 1870's. Most men caried their gun in a pocket of their "sack" coat, a lose fitting short coat, or in the waistband of their pants.

Courtney's Irish Luck Runs Out

This marked the end of the Morgan Courtney legend. Five of McKinney's shots hit Courtney — one in front and four into his back. His fine linen coat had even caught fire due to the close-range shots. Several witnesses testified that the two men could not have been more than three to four feet apart when the first shot was fired.

The only description we have of Georgie Scyphers was picked up from *The Eureka Sentinel*, September 24, 1873,

> "Her face was a pleasing one; and her [sic], language, dress, and actions in court, little betokened the life she was leading; and many were almost moved to pity her. She was plainly dressed in black. She testified as follows in reply to questions, 'I knew Morgan Courtney and the defendant. I had a conversation with the defendant about Mr. Courtney whilst the latter was living. On the evening of the shooting, I had a very little conversation with Mr. McKinney; I also saw him in the morning. I had promised to go to Mr. McKinney's room in the evening. He asked me why I didn't come, and I said it was because I was afraid of Mr. Courtney. As I arose to leave the room, I think, well I know —the remark he made was that he would wring my heart with the .... [sic] before I would ever be with him again.... he said he

hated him because other people feared him.
…. I saw that pistol, or one like it, that night
in the hands of the defendant".

Witness, James Finley, testified per *the Pioche Daily Record*, September 14, 1873, that when Courtney was in the Drug store and dying, he said first, "I'm gone," and then said that McKinney shot him and "Thank God it will soon be over."

After being told that he was not going to recover, Courtney dictated a statement:

> "I think I'm going to die. I was walking down the street and McKinney shot me in the back. I started to run in order to get in a place to defend myself, but he shot so fast that I could not do anything but run. I did not shoot at McKinney at all. I did not get my pistol out until he fired six shots…." *"Pioche Daily Record,"* September 14, 1873.

The statement was written on a torn piece of wrapping paper and was witnessed by John Wilson, K.J. Hanley, John Manning, O.C. Mc Donald, and James Finley. Courtney died the next day, August 2[n], 1873, about noon.

When the physicians went to make a post-mortem examination of the body, William Kelly had arrived and declared that he was a cousin of the deceased. He stopped the examination and warned that he would shoot the first man who put a knife in the dead body. He seemed to appear out of nowhere at the death scene and quickly took charge of the action. A post-mortem is basically a limited autopsy and it

142

appeared that William Kelly felt that this would be a desecration of his cousin's body, and that the honorable thing to do was to stop it — which he did. He then claimed the body, made the funeral arrangements, and was appointed by the court as executor of Courtney's Will. No one involved questioned the kinship. William Kelly was also in the Gold Hill, Nevada, directory in 1868, the same time that Courtney was in Gold Hill. I do believe that they were cousins and had been in touch with one another since both entered the U.S.

"Georgie Scyphers was called to the Drug store to make a statement. When she finished, she walked over to the corpse and fainted. When she recovered, she left the room quickly and weeping bitterly." "Pioche Daily Record," August 3, 1873.

The luck of the Irish had finally run out.

Mark Twain in his book "Roughing It" sums up the life of the legendary gunfighter this way,

> "They were brave, reckless men, and traveled with their lives in their hands. To give them their due, they did their killing principally among themselves, and seldom molested peaceable citizens, for they considered it small credit to add to their trophy so cheap a bauble as the death of a man who was 'not on the shoot,' as they phrased it. They killed each other on slight provocation and hoped and expected to be killed themselves…for they held it almost shame to die otherwise than 'with their boots on,' as they expressed it." [38]

Boot Hill #186

On Sunday, August 3rd, at 3:00 o clock, the funeral procession for Rick Moriarty/Morgan Courtney convened on Main Street led by Father Monteverde and Courtney's cousin, William J. Kelly, riding together in a buggy.

Following next were the American Brass Band, the Hook and Ladder Company, the hearse, accompanied by ten pallbearers, the Hose Company and then citizens — some on foot, others in carriages or on horseback. The entire procession numbered over 300 people, extending over a half mile.

The procession moved up Cedar Street to the Catholic Church, then to Meadow Valley Street and turned down Main Street to the graveyard. Morgan Courtney was buried in the famous Boot Hill graveyard — # 186.

The editor of the *"Pioche Daily Record,"* August 3, 1873, summed up Morgan Courtney's life in an article entitled,

> "The Lesson of the Hour" .... "Morgan Courtney, alias Rick Moriarty, is numbered among the dead. It is sad to reflect that one so young, so qualified to adorn some honorable station, should have been so suddenly cut off and pushed into the presence of his Maker....Morgan Courtney (the name by which he was known in this community), feared by some, detested by others and

respected by a few, was a desperate character — he killed his man in Pioche some fourteen months ago — a murder in the broadest exception of the term.

What he may have done before is not a proper question for discussion at this time. Suffice it to say that God Almighty, who tempers justice with his mercy has already dealt with Morgan Courtney. We only refer to his death as a verification of the prophecy that those who slay by the sword, shall by the sword be slain.

The notoriously bad character of Courtney gave no immunity to McKinney to slay him like a dog. McKinney is himself a low order of man. The writer knew him in Virginia in the Fall of 1871, has known him in Pioche for some months and has never known him to do a day's work to keep soul and body together. He is the man who tried to commit suicide in Virginia some months ago but failed in the attempt.

Of the prompting cause for the shooting of Courtney, we are not advised. Certain as it is that McKinney had no license from God or man to slay him. Courtney's death sows the feeling in this community. There were those in Pioche who feared and consequently pretended to respect him. There are men who exulted over the acquittal of Courtney for the brutal murder of Sullivan who now rejoices that he died with his boots on. We are not dealing in sentimentality. Morgan Courtney has met the fate due his crime.

Let McKinney meet a righteous doom. It is fortunate that no quiet orderly citizen had been murdered as Courtney was, for in that case the people would have avenged his death by summarily hanging the assassin. Poor Courtney, while there were those who were willing to swear to anything to screen him from the gallows and are now laughing in their sleeves at his tragic end, we pity him. May God have mercy on the soul of Morgan Courtney, may justice and law deal with is cowardly assassin."

The Pioche Daily Record, Aug. 8, 1873, reported:

"The Community loses nothing by the death of Courtney, and should McKinney be hung for his assassination, the whole affair will be one of congratulation to the people of Pioche."

On September 20th, after a ten-day trial, the jury deliberated three minutes before acquitting McKinney due to Courtney's threats and his defamatory language — the same reasons for the acquittal of Courtney in the Sullivan case. It's alleged that shortly after the acquittal McKinney left town with Georgie Scyphers. He evidently overcame his laudanum addiction and intestinal problems and lived into the next century. Georgie Scyphers disappeared completely — maybe got married; maybe changed her name.

This seems like a logical ending to a book about the life of Morgan Courtney, but just like his life, there remains one more twist and turn.

Manning Seeks Revenge

Giddy... up —Gee!

John Manning had become friends with Courtney over a period of ten years when Courtney was still known as Richard Moriarty. They had met on a sailing ship from New Zealand to British Columbia. They had mined together there, and then had reconnected in Idaho and were together the night that one of them shot the innocent Chinese woman, and then again in Gold Hill, Virginia City, and Pioche. They had both been forced to immigrate from Ireland. They had traveled from place to place for years as young men without family. It's easy to understand that their bond would have been as clansmen to the Irish and like brothers to you and me.

John Manning was a material witness at the Sullivan trial, at the McKinney trial, and was with Courtney at his death. It's understandable that Manning was totally distraught at the loss of his clansman and best friend.

After Courtney's death, the town became polarized over the killing. Some of Courtney's friends collected funds to help the District Attorney hire extra counsel to convict McKinney, and McKinney had his own following who were financing his defense. The Courtney camp felt that Deputy Sheriff McKee had played a part in setting up Courtney's death, and Manning especially felt that McKee was one of Sheriff

Travis' "pets" and had been complicit in the ensuing gun fight which took Courtney's life.

A month later, Manning, James Wales, James Hunter, and O'Brien were drinking heavily one night, fighting and brandishing weapons. Early the next morning, Deputy McKee cornered three of the group and disarmed them for their own safety, but Manning was not there at the time.

Hunter, in a moment of clarity, did caution the deputy, a large man, known in town as "Fat Mac" that Manning blamed him for Courtney's death. Within a short while, McKee was walking down Main Street and Manning approached saying. "Hold on Mac, I think you're a friend of the party that killed Courtney."[39]

Mac replied, "What have you got to say about it."

"Nothing, Mac, but I don't like officers that murder a man."

"You are drunk now. Any difference we have had we will settle when you are sober. Go to bed, and when you get sober, I'll talk to you."

"Mac, there's no damned son of a bitch in this town can make me go to bed. I'll go to bed when I'm ready."

Manning made a move for his gun but was still under the influence of last night's liquor. Fat Mac, sober and on duty, drew faster, fired, and hit Manning with the first shot. Also, it should be noted that Deputy McKee was carrying a double action pistol which could be fired without cocking the hammer. Manning was carrying a single action pistol which had to be cocked. This also was a factor in McKee getting the first shot.

Manning was taken to the drug store, where his boots were removed. This must have been done out of respect for Manning, as he was not perpetrating a cold-blooded murder. He was trying to avenge the death of his good friend. We note that this act of taking the boots off, apparently, was not done for Courtney.

Manning died within a half hour and was the 192nd person buried in the Boot Hill Cemetery.

Now the shooting left poor Deputy McKee in a bad predicament. Amazingly, he was arrested for murder, and the bail was set at $10,000. However, the grand jury refused to move forward with an indictment, which seemed the right thing to do in the law-challenged town of Pioche. As usual, the townspeople moved on quickly, and a year later Fat Mac was elected to Pioche Constable and later to County Sheriff.

Manning was given a proper funeral attended by about 150 people, but it was a quiet funeral. The townsmen of Pioche were starting to tire of the gunfighting crowd and the continued violence on Main Street. One of the local Paiutes remarked, "White man hep kill 'em too much in Pioche."[40]

It was time for Pioche to grow up and become a regular family town— full of miners and shopkeepers working hard for a day's pay to support their families. Pioche did grow up and successfully produce multiple generations of native sons and daughters — some who became miners, but also teachers, nurses, lawyers, electricians, engineers, entrepreneurs, policemen, hairdressers, waitresses and even writers, who continue to enrich the State of Nevada with their hard rock mining heritage.

Postscript

Morgan Courtney died in August of 1873, and by the last half of that year mining in Pioche had started to decline — the average number of recorded mining claims had dropped to about 25% of that in 1872. In 1874, the shaft of the Raymond and Ely mine was down to over 1,000 feet and their stock was dropping significantly. In March, the miners struck water at the 1200 feet level, which virtually was the end of the first boom in Pioche. Prospectors, claim jumpers, merchants, gamblers, and gunfighters were moving on to Arizona, Death Valley, and southwestern Colorado.

Below are a few final thoughts on the people we've met on this journey so far...

Richard Moriarty aka Morgan Courtney – This man was most certainly not a person you or I would want to invite to dinner, but was he a sociopath or maybe a psychopath? I think a good case could be made for either diagnosis; however, I am not qualified to make that judgement. I can only say that he was, without a doubt, a product of his environment and circumstances — the great Irish famine; the life of an immigrant in a country where the Irish were not valued, and sometimes despised; and the vagaries of the gold mining industry along with the lawlessness which this industry fostered during these eras. If you combined these circumstances with the personality of a child who needed to be noticed and in charge, you just might come up with an adult who decided that life would be better if he was the bully.

I was always curious throughout my research of Richard, as to his educational background. I knew that during the mid-1800's that Gaelic was the spoken language, but it was very evident during the Morgan Courtney court trials that Richard had a great command of the English language. How did this happen, I wondered? I learned that after 1691, Catholics were not permitted to have schools, or own land or a house. During this extended period, the English did operate some private schools (too expensive for the Irish), but the Irish started operating "hedge schools" for their own children. These were virtual outdoor schools nestled near the hedges where the children would not be noticed, and they were taught by Irish teachers.

In the 1840's, the English instituted national education in Ireland, but all classes had to be taught in the English language — a second language for the Irish children. I can only assume that Richard was able to be taught in a national school, and that he had, indeed, excelled in learning English. I hope to be able to one day confirm this information.

Georgianne "Georgie" Cyphers – No book about a gunfighter should be written without the entrance of a local prostitute, and this book is no exception. However, I was not optimistic about finding any factual background about Georgie. Prostitutes came and went in all mining camps and usually left no traces. They often married and changed their names, but rarely stayed long with the same man, making it very difficult to pin down their identity when they moved on to the next bonanza or significant other.

The Pioche newspapers printed Georgie's last name as "Scyphers" and a few other variations, but always beginning with a "S." However, several newspaper articles appeared in Google searches which offered additional information on Georgie. *The Eureka Daily Sentinel*, January 24, 1873, reported, "Mr. Cypher and wife are on the passenger list from Hamilton to Pioche. The temperature in that family must always be a "0." In decimal fractions their value may be represented thus: .01."

It appears that the wife in this article must be Georgie, and she was at that time married to James Byron Cyphers. *The Pioche Daily Record*, April 18, 1873, shows James V. Cyphers leaving Pioche on April 16, 1873, for Salt Lake City by himself. It appears that Mr. and Mrs. Cyphers arrived in Pioche in January of 1873, a few months prior to Courtney's arrival, and possibly had separated, with James leaving Pioche without Georgie several months later.

January 12, 1876, *Pioche Daily Record* reports that Jimmy Cyphers arrived at Mrs. Nuttell's house in Salt Lake City injured from multiple gunshot wounds, allegedly inflicted by Mexican bandits. The chambers of Cypher's revolver were empty, and he was not expected to live. He was referred to as formerly one of the boys in Salt Lake. Was Jimmy Cyphers also a gunfighter, and was it possible that Georgie had parted from one gunfighter in Pioche, to take up company with two others, Morgan Courtney and James McKinney?

The Carson City Morning Appeal reported August 6, 1878, that Georgie Syphers [sic] had shot a man at Belleville, and that "This woman indirectly caused the death of a man in Pioche, and another who resides near Bodie was wounded on her account."

This is where the trail of Georgianne Cyphers ends. I suspect another name change occurred after the above report. By the way, up to this time, Georgie had escaped indictment on each of these shooting incidents.

Deputy William McKee stayed on in Pioche and was elevated to Sheriff in 1876, serving until 1882. He took a wife in 1875, Malissa Radford, age 14, from Milford, Utah. Pioche is about 50 miles from the Utah border. At some point they separated or divorced, and the Sheriff married again in 1880, to Lizzie (last name not published), age 19, also from Milford, Utah. *The Eureka Daily Sentinel*, February 24, 1882, reported, "McKee, better known as 'Fat McKee;' figured conspicuously as a police officer in the 'rough days' of Pioche. He was about the only officer in those times whom the bad element feared and dreaded. He was a very powerful man physically, and though quite fleshy — whence his nickname — was remarkably quick and very active, considering his size. In making arrests he was frequently, but never successfully, resisted."

Sheriff McKee prevented more crimes than those that occurred, saving numerous lives. He died in 1882, at age 47, of bronchitis and was buried in Boot Hill.

George W. McKinney, according to the 1870 census records for Elko, Nevada, was born about 1848 in

Ohio, which made him 25 years old at the time of the Courtney shoot out. He listed his occupation as a "saddler" — which was, evidently, prior to becoming a noted night watchman, fast with a six sooter. He had attempted suicide in Virginia City two years previously. After his acquittal subsequent to the Courtney shooting, he left the area with Georgie Cyphers, and was rumored to have recovered from his medical maladies and lived many years. There is no indication that he and Georgie married or stayed together.

William J. Kelly, appeared at the scene of Courtney's death, introducing himself as Courtney's cousin. He declared to the Sheriff that Courtney's given name was Richard Moriarty, and that Richard's parents were still living in Caharsiveen, Ireland, (but he gave no names.) Kelly took possession of the body, planned the funeral, and handled Richard's estate.

The Carson Daily Appeal reported July 9, 1873, one month prior to Courtney's death that, "Yesterday morning about 8 o'clock Wm. J. Kelly and Joseph Kennedy had a difficulty in front of Waterhouse's saloon on Main Street. It appears that the parties had some trouble the evening before at the Cosmopolitan Saloon and, meeting in the morning, some words passed between them, when Kennedy, who was considerably under the influence of liquor, started for Kelly, who pulled out his six-shooter and fired two shots, one of them taking effect in the left groin of Kennedy, inflicting an ugly looking but fortunately not severe wound. The parties were separated, and Kelly immediately walked up to the Sheriff's office and gave himself up. An examination of the case was held before Justice Logan this afternoon which resulted in the discharge of Kelly." So, evidently, William Kelly, was also earning his money as a gunfighter and/or a watchman at one of the local mines in Pioche at the same time as his cousin, Richard Moriarty aka Morgan Courtney.

Three years later we find a report from the Austin, Nevada, Police Department records for August 6, 1876. Kelly had become a deputy sheriff in Austin and was killed on the job: "Deputy Kelly was stabbed to death by a woman who was involved in a quarrel at the racetrack in Austin, Nevada. The woman was fighting with another woman and Deputy Kelly intervened. After the races, Deputy Kelly encountered the woman a second time in front of a saloon on Cedar Street. During the encounter, the woman stabbed Deputy Kelly in the chest. Although mortally wounded, Deputy Kelly was able to shoot the woman in the leg. Deputy Kelly died minutes later. The woman was taken into custody, but the outcome of the incident is not known."

James Moriarty was living at the Loon Creek Mining District of central Idaho, according to the 1870 census., with four other Irish placer miners. He listed himself as single and "cannot read or write."

In 1872, he became a naturalized U.S. citizen, and by 1880, had served as an Express agent for Wells Fargo, covering stagecoach lines in Utah, Idaho, and Oregon, and had been elected Auditor and Recorder of the County. In addition, he also had opened a clothing store in Boise, offering clothing, hats, caps, etc., and later was written up in an Idaho Historical

Review as a founding father. (I wonder if Richard Moriarty aka Morgan Courtney had purchased his fine suits and shirts from the Moriarty Clothing store in Boise, Idaho?)

By the 1900 census, James was 62 years old, had given up the store, and listed himself in the census as a gold quartz miner. He is shown living with two nephews: Patrick Moriarty, age 38, and James Moriarty Jr., age 43, and a niece Kate Moriarty. Patrick had immigrated in 1883, from Caherdaniel, a neighboring village to Cahersiveen, as had James Jr. who had immigrated in 1873. Both nephews listed their occupation as quartz miners, and both could read and write English.

On January 19, 1906, all three of the Moriarty men were working at the Boulder Quartz Mill in Elk Creek. At about 9:30 that morning James Sr. had started shoveling a heavy, wet snow off the roof of the mill. James Jr. had warned him that the snow was not in good condition to be shoveled, and he had returned into the mine tunnel. James Sr. started shoveling regardless of the warning. At about noon, the two nephews came out of the tunnel to find that the snow had slid from the roof and buried James Sr. He had died instantly.

At his funeral it was stated that, "Many a miner and prospector would have gone hungry but for the kindness of Mr. Moriarty. He acquired the reputation of being altogether too liberal for a successful hotel man."[41] James Sr. did not marry, nor did either of the nephews or the niece, so there are no descendants with further information on that branch of the Moriarty family.

The Weapons – The Chinese started experimenting during the 9th century with a combination of saltpeter, charcoal, and Sulphur, resulting in black powder, which they tamped into bamboo shoots and metal tubes—creating the first guns. This invention was immediately used for protection and was traded along the silk road, making its way to Europe and to the Americas. Each war from then on provided the impetus and the money to fund further refinements to all firearms and cannons.

By the mid 1860's, the time of the western gold and silver rush, pistols and rifles had become readily available due to a marked increase in manufacturing during the Civil War. Between 1848 and 1873, the Colt Company turned out 21,000 revolvers, known as "Revolving horse pistols." Many of which found their way to the California gold camps. Further advancements were made by the Colt Company, and 200,500, (1860) Colt Army revolvers were produced for the Civil War. Thousands of these guns made their way west after the end of the war, as soldiers were allowed to purchase them directly from the Army. Also, Smith and Wesson introduced a popular single action six shooter in 1870.

The introduction of the vest pocket Deringer was a real game changer. In fact, this was the gun used by John Wilkes Booth to assassinate President Lincoln. It could more easily be concealed in clothing than any other gun on the market. Contrary to Hollywood movies, almost all revolvers were carried in pockets or waist bands, as holsters were not reliably usable until the 1920's.

During the Civil War, soldiers took great pride in owning a Henry Rifle, often called "sixteen shooters," because the chamber held that many rounds. Many infantry soldiers purchased a Henry with their re-enlistment bonus, as they figured the Henry's high rate of fire could save their lives. Historians argue that one man armed with a Henry was equivalent to 14 or 15 men equipped with single-shot guns. It's not hard to figure how valuable a Henry would be to any man living in Nevada during the mid-1800's.

The most versatile and economical firearm for hunting and defense was the twin-barreled scatter gun, used by ranchers, stagecoach guards "riding shotgun," and lawmen. The best balanced and favorite six-shooter of its time was the Colt single action army revolver released in 1873, which became an instant favorite with lawmen, settlers, and bandits. As we've mentioned before, there was a fine line between these three classes on the frontier.

In 1873, the *Pioche Record* noted, "A man sneezed in the presence of another yesterday, and the other did not even draw his Whistler..." Edward Whistler had just released his new English patent pistol which had become the rage in Pioche — a very fast six-shooter, which could release all six rounds in rapid succession.

In short, many male residents of Pioche owned one of the above guns, but certainly not more than one. Guns were expensive, ranging from $2.50 to $3.00 and upwards to $10.00 for a special model. Therefore, when a man arrived in Pioche with a

Henry rifle and a six shooter, all eyes looked his direction, as it was a sure sign that another "gunfighter" had arrived.

Courtney's Guns – One day a package arrived on our doorstep, which my husband handed to me and said, "This is gift from me; don't be mad." Imagine my surprise! I now owned an 1860 Colt Army 44 Caliber six-shooter, and since I am a lifelong pacifist, I was shocked, to say the least. However, I had chosen to write a book about a gunfighter, so what could I say but, "Thank you!" Now, I must say that over time I have become quite fond of my six-shooter, because it's a real beauty.

It's 11 inches from hammer to end of the barrel and weighs about two pounds. Of course, it is totally safe because it doesn't use bullets. You load all six chambers from the front "muzzle" end. Paper cartridges were used which consisted of pre-measured loads of black powder and a small lead ball, wrapped in a paper that was soaked in potassium nitrate and then dried.

To load, you slipped this wrapped concoction into the chamber and tamped it into place with the lever ram (located below the barrel) and then placed a percussion cap at the back end of the chamber. This process was repeated another five times to load all six chambers. Therefore, if you needed more than six shots in a waged battle, you better have a second loaded gun handy. Maybe this is where the Henry rifle comes in — I must declare that I refuse to own one of those!

I stared at my gun off and on for several months, hesitating to handle it, during which time my husband never said a word to me — he knew better. One day, my curiosity got the best of me, and I decided to seriously examine the various mechanisms of my six-shooter. Then I went looking for a coat with deep pockets. I came up with a raincoat that falls just below the hips and with fairly deep pockets, but the opening of the pockets run up and down instead of across the front of the coat. That, however, was the best I could do at that moment, so I proceeded to place my gun into one of the pockets. The gun is actually 15 inches from end of muzzle to end of handle, so the entire handle was visible — my weapon was not concealed — Oh geeze! I then tried to pull the gun out quickly. It caught slightly on the edges of the pocket. In other words, if I had been in a gun fight, I would be dead.

I raised my arm to shoulder height and carefully aimed in a safe direction. I could hold the gun steady, with effort, but probably not steady enough to hit a target. However, I had observed that the 1870's gun fighters seemed to be picking targets three to six feet away — now I understood why.

Holsters – As explained previously, holsters were not used widely by gunfighters until the 1920's. They existed, but the leather was tough and not conducive to a "fast draw." The shootout at the O.K. Corral occurred in 1881. A quote from Tom Clavin's book, "*Tombstone*," gives us a good view of this famous gun fight. "Tom McLaury tossed open his coat, apparently to grab one or perhaps two guns. There might well be shooting after all. Wyatt pulled his gun out of his right coat pocket. Doc yanked the shotgun up out of his coat and pulled the hammers back. There was a sudden 'click-click' from either the shotgun or the hammers of two pistols being drawn back — and the sound was especially loud in the hushed silence of the vacant lot."[42] The ever-popular sack coat and a longer version worn by Doc Holliday were the gun receptacles of the day in the 1870's and early 80's.

Boots – Most men in 1870, had only one pair of boots, so your boots were well recognizable by others, much like a winter parka would be today. If you were a stagecoach robber you would, of course, cover your face with a bandana during the robbery, but what about your boots? Hmmm…what to do? The answer is, the robbers tied gunny sacks over their boots prior to robbing a stage, to be easily removed after the fast get-a-way.

Gunfighter (as a term) – I have chosen to use the term "gunfighter" throughout this book. It seemed to be the best choice for describing Courtney and the other characters who were living by the gun, and it was a term used by Bat Masterson. This term was also interchangeable for those who were hired legally as watchmen or as sheriffs. The term "gunslinger" was coined in the 1920's by writers of western novels and movie scripts. Other authentic terms used during the 1870's were: "gunmen," "pistoleers," "shootist" or "badman."

Faro — Gaming In The 1800's

Are you ready to play? The King is the highest card, and the Ace the lowest.

The banker will turn two cards over at a time. In the meantime, the players have placed their chips (betting) on one or more cards showing on the board. The dealer turns over the first card, which becomes the loser. The dealer takes all the chips off the board for that number. The second card turned up is the winner, and the dealer pays one to one to the players who bet on that number.

This process continues with the dealer moving through the deck, two cards per hand. Therefore, if you can count cards, you can increase your odds as to which card the dealer will turn over on the next play.

Then, when you get that figured out, you can place a penny on your chip and bet that the next card turned over will be higher than the second card turned over and other similar variations — basically you are making side bets with your penny. Legend has it that the last Faro game was dealt at the Ramada Casino in Reno, which closed in 1985.

Notes

[1] Clavin, Tom, "Tombstone," St. Martins Press 2020

[2] "That is good, it squeaks": Charles Gracey, "Early Days in Lincoln County, (Nevada Historical Society)

[3] "That ore might have lain there": Ibid.

[4] "If either of them set foot": Ibid

[5] "We will drive those fellows off": Ibid.

[6] "Morgan Courtney turned out to be a sport": Ibid.

[7] Shumway, Corinne Fullerton & Hone, Peggy Draper, "I Dig Pioche", (The Pioche Historical Society)

[8] Fullerton-Shumway & Draper-Hone

[9] "Since my last visit": Leo Schafer, "Boot Hill, the Pioche cemetery", Book Connection, LLC., Pioche Nevada 2008

[10] "Given a little time": Fullerton-Shumway and Draper-Hone, Op. Cit.

[11] "He prided himself in ordering": Charles Convis, "Outlaw Tales of Nevada", Morris Book Publishing; LLC – 2006, 1st ed. 1926.

[12] "The desperado stalked": Mark Twain, Roughing it…

[13] "It is now agreed, at least": Com Toibin and Diarmaid Ferriter, "The Irish Famine", Profile Books

[14] "Coffins were now becoming scarce": Asenath Nicholson, "Annals of the Famine in Ireland in

1847, 1848 & 1849", Books Ulter, 2017 1st ed.
1851.

[15] "Minorities were the norm": Richard Thomas Wright, "Barkerville and the Cariboo Goldfields", Heritage House Publishing Company, Ltd., 2013

[16] "Many, if not most women": Ibid

[17] "But then, there were the Hurdy dancers": Ibid.

[18] "Hurdy Gurdy Damsels": Ibid

[19] "What was your name in the States": Ibid

[20] "We immediately sunk a hole": "The Gold Camps and Silver Cities of Idaho", Bureau of Mines 1963

[21] "Nothing was on the level": Effie Mona Mack, "Mark Twain in Nevada", Charles Scribner's Sons, 1947

[22] "Little stacks of gold and silver": Ronald M. James, "The Roar and the Silence", University of Nevada Press, Reno NV 1998

[23] "Vice flourished luxuriantly": Ibid.

[24] "He said he had come from Salt Lake City", Convis, Op. Cit

[25] "Tom Kirby, who had been herding ", Convis, Op. Cit.

[26] "Up the canyon from the west": Neill C. Wilson, "Silver Stampede", The Rio Grande Press, Inc. Glorieta, New Mexico, 1987 1st ed. 1937

[27] "On his arrival he handed": Schafer, Op. Cit.

[28] "If you don't take it, you're": State of Nevada vs. Morgan Courtney

[29] "When Sullivan was carried": Ibid.

[30] "Any man who does not possess courage": W.B. Masterson (Bat), "Famous Gunfighters of The Western Frontier", Digireads.com, 2020

[31] "Was not the first remark of Sullivan": State of Nevada, Op. Cit.

[32] "I had eight or ten drinks at the theatre": State of Nevada, Op. Cit.

[33] "I was in Pioche on the 8th of June last": State of Nevada, Op. Cit.

[34] "I saw the body lying there", State of Nevada, Op. Cit.

[35] "I have known Morgan Courtney ever since": State of Nevada, Op. Cit.

[36] "The better citizens of this place, Leo Schafer, Op. Cit.

[37] "Mr. Courtney will not be Chief anymore": Gracy Op. Cit.

[38] "They were brave, reckless men": Twain, Op. Cit.

[39] "Hold on Mac": Schafer, Op. Cit.

[40] "Whiteman hep kill 'em too much": Schafer, Op. Cit.

[41] "Many a miner and prospector": Family History by Mary Ellen.blogspost.com/2013/05

[42] "Tom McLaury tossed open his coat": Clavin, Op. Cit.

Boot hill. Pioche, Nv

1863 Colt Army .44 Cal.

Court Drawing of Richard Moriarty aka Morgan

Courtney

Main Street, Pioche

Freight Wagon

Well Fargo Stage Coach

Pioche Bar Scene

Part III James H. Leavy

Gunfighter

James Leavy Joins The Pioche Roughs

In 1870, the population of Nevada was 42,491, and of that figure approximately 30,000 folks lived in the Virginia City area. Therefore, roughly 12,500 people populated the entire remaining vastness of Nevada.

Those 12,500 seemed to be mounted on wheels, as there was an endless amount of traffic between the various mining camps. Miners are a restless lot by nature and are prone to drop everything and take off to the next glory hole at a moment's notice. So, as my research continued, I was pleased, but not terribly surprised, when I discovered that one of my gunfighter characters had shown up at the same camp and had become a good friend of another gunfighting character.

Also, the witness of one shooting, which I had written about, suddenly appeared as a witness of a subsequent shooting. What are the chances, I wondered, but I didn't live in Pioche in the 1870's! In Part I of this book a foursome of trained gunfighters clear out a nest of claim jumpers at the Raymond and Ely mine in Pioche. Two chapters later, we learn that Michael Casey, one of the four gunfighters, gets into an altercation with a Mr. Gorson, a man to whom he is indebted due to a mining property transaction.

Before Gorson died of his gunshot wounds, he executed a Will, leaving assets to various friends and stipulating that $5,000 be distributed to the man who kills his assailant, Casey. James Leavy, a young

Pioche miner, was on Main Street the day of the shooting and had witnessed the murder of Gorson who was his friend. Casey, of course, had claimed self-defense, but Leavy testified that he saw the shooting and that Casey had, in fact, fired the first shot.

Leavy then calculated that he was in a good position to go after the $5,000 reward money. After all, he was a witness to the murder of Gorson, and he would be vindicating the wrongful death of a friend. If there was a reward involved, why should it not be him? So Leavy proclaimed vociferously in several of the Pioche saloons that he witnessed the murder, and that Casey had shot Gorson without warning. These were fightin' words in Pioche, without question!

Charles Gracey, Pioche resident, and engineer for Raymond and Ely mine, reported the incident this way:

> "I knew Levy [sic] well. He was a very quiet man and a good miner and worked every day. Casey met Levy [sic] in Freudenthal's store and in my presence asked Levy if he had indeed said that Casey fired the first shot. Levy said that he had and was ready to swear to it. Casey then commenced abusing Levy. Levy replied in a quiet way: 'You can abuse me now while you have your gun with you.' Levy had just come from his work in the mine and carried his lunch bucket in his hand. Casey told him to get his gun and come shooting[43]."

[44]"Levy left the store, went to his cabin, changed his clothes, got his gun and returned. Dave Nagel [sic], another miner was on the sidewalk in front of Freudenthal's store watching for Levy to come back along the street, but Levy came through an alley instead which ran alongside the store, and thus surprised Casey and Nagel."

Leavy then fired at Casey, grazing his skull. Casey dove at Leavy, and Leavy fired, shooting Casey in the neck. As Casey fell to the ground, Leavy struck Casey in the head with his pistol.

> Gracey then states, "The shooting commenced at once. Nagel ran out into the street and fired several shots at Levy . But Levy and Casey had clinched and were on the sidewalk together. I think now and have always thought that it was the beating over the head with a pistol that killed Casey rather than the shots that were fired. Nagel hit Levy in the lower jaw or chin and made a bad scar.[45]"

Neagle had, in fact, shot Leavy in the jaw area which left disfiguring holes in both cheeks. The Sheriff, John Pattie, arrested both Neagle and Leavy and locked them in the same cell until they each posted bail. Leavy returned to his room at the Hamilton's lodging and was treated by Dr. Folz for his wound. He was initially in critical condition with a fractured jaw and holes in both cheeks. Neagle's bullet did leave him with a sinister looking scar, which remained with him the rest of his life. There was a large funeral for Casey attended by 250 people.

Gracey further reports: "Casey's friends now were the enemies of Levy and tried their best to kill him. But he proved to be the most fearless and aggressive in that line that had ever appeared and was soon the terror of all the fighters[46]."

David Neagle was charged with shooting Leavy but was discharged by a Grand Jury. Leavy eventually collected the $5,000 reward left by Gorson. At a court hearing, it was decided that Leavy had given Casey fair warning that he was coming after him with a gun, "heeled," so it was a "Pioche-style" fair fight. Leavy was immediately released from further prosecution. One man dead, one man wounded, three shooters and no need for prosecution — a typical court day in Pioche!

America — The Land Of The Free

James H. Leavy was born in Dublin, Ireland, about 1842, the beginning of the Irish famine, and within two years of the birth of Richard Moriarty, his gunfighting idol. Dublin, the capital of Ireland is located on the Dublin Bay, a c-shaped inlet of the Irish sea which separates Ireland from Great Britain, part of the greater Atlantic Ocean.

Richard Moriarty was born on the southwest coast of Ireland, in Cahersiveen, 229 miles from Dublin. Even though all of Ireland was affected by the famine, the population of southwest Ireland was completely decimated. There were more soup kitchens in Dublin, but many people, especially in the middle to lower classes, were starving and the death toll was very high.

In May of 1852, Thomas Leavy, James' father, who was listed on a ship's manifest as a laborer, had survived the worst of the famine, but was still struggling to make a living for his family. He made the huge decision to emigrate to America with his two sons, James, age ten, and John, age six. Did Thomas have a wife and other children? We just don't know. Many Irish split their families when they emigrated thinking that the strongest could survive the ocean passage, get jobs in America, and quickly send money back to support the rest of the family. This is the ubiquitous plan of most immigrants everywhere in the world — it's a plan of survival for every family caught up in "mass migration."

Was Mrs. Leavy deceased or did she stay behind with smaller children? There are too many people with similar names to be able to trace the entire family. However, since there is no mention of his mother in any other source, I think that it is probable that she died in Ireland, and Thomas decided that his two sons would have a chance for a better life in America rather than remaining in the famine-torn homeland.

The father and two sons boarded a ship of the Huguenot line, better known during the famine as a "coffin ship" from Liverpool, Great Britain, and docked in the harbor of New York City, May 14, 1852. The threesome would have headed immediately to the Five Points area of the city, the immigrant village of New York, where they could quickly locate Irish clansmen who would help them find food and housing.

In the late 1700's, there was a small lake located in New York City southwest of Bunker Hill, known as "The Collect." It had become a favored location for slaughterhouses and tanneries — a place where those industries could use the water for disposal of their waste products. By the end of the century, The Collect had become a putrid nuisance, and the city's population had advanced toward the north.

In 1802, the City Council ordered the Collect to be backfilled, and simultaneously leveled Bunker Hill, creating a new area for development by local landowners such as the Ashdors, later known as the Astors. Anthony Street had been extended east to the intersection of Orange and Cross Streets, completing a five-corner intersection, quickly to be known as

"Five Points." Developers filled this area with two-and-a half-story wooden buildings —the half story was an attic with low ceilings and dormer windows. These buildings were initially rented to local artisans who maintained shops for their wares on the ground floor and lived above the shop in small apartments.

By the 1830's, immigration was increasing so rapidly that landowners began dividing the two-story houses into small apartments in order to rent the same space to multiple families. As time went on, the houses were divided again, creating more apartments per square foot, and the houses started to be referred to as "tenement houses."

In time it became apparent that the backfilled swamp under the tenements had remained damp and unstable, which was causing the houses to shift and tilt. The basements would flood at the first drop of rain or snow. This, accompanied by poor infrastructure for sewage, as, initially, there was no infrastructure (out-houses only) created the huge cholera epidemic of 1832, during which thousands of New Yorkers lost their lives. The immigrants were readily blamed for the epidemic citing their "desolate living habits," with no mention of the true underlying causes.

By 1834, the press started to investigate the Five Points area and published numerous exposes. One reporter found,

> "That apartments in the worst parts of Five Points did not have a 'table, chair or any other article of furniture, save a cooking utensil, a few plates, and knives, and bottles, with which

to carry on the business of living. Few beds were found in any of these apartments, the inmates sleeping or lying on heaps of filthy rags, straw and shavings, the stench from which was almost insupportable....In the afternoon of each day, when drunkenness is at its height, the most disgusting objects , of both sexes, are exhibited to the eyes of the examiner. Indecency, squalid poverty, intemperance and crime, riot and revel in continued orgies, and sober humanity is shocked and horrified, at the loathsome spectacles incessantly presented."[47]

At 37 ½ Baxter Street, government inspectors discovered in one of the stuffy, windowless bedrooms the widow, Honora Moriarty, and her teenaged daughters, Margaret and Mary, undoubtedly from County Kerry, southwest Ireland. (County Kerry was the main location of the Moriarty clan.) Many Kerry immigrants had been relocated by the owners of the Lansdowne estate during the famine, who elected to pay their tenants' passage to America, rather than try to feed them on the estate.

"The old dame of sixty and her two daughters, the legislators reported in horror, supported themselves by picking curled hair out of city garbage barrels and then selling it to wigmakers or other manufacturers. By scouring the streets sixteen hours a day, they managed to find enough hair to earn five dollars per week[48]."

By the 1830's, Five Points was so well known for its depravities that tourists flocked to the area to witness the debauchery for themselves. Davy Crockett published "*An Account of Col. Crockett's tour to the North and Down East*," where he lists Five Points as one of the high-lights of his trip:

> "The buildings are little, old, frame houses, and looked like some little country village…It appeared as if the cellars was jam full of people, and such fiddling and dancing nobody ever saw before in this world. The mixing of the races in these dance halls. was especially noteworthy: Black and white, white and black, all 'hugemsnug' together, happy as lords and ladies, sitting sometimes round in a ring, with a jug of liquor between them: and I do think I saw more drunk folks, men and women, that day, than I ever saw before…..I thought I would rather risqué myself in an Indian fight than venture among these creatures after night. Crowds of elites from other parts of New York started venturing into 'Five Points' to observe the night life, coining the phrase of 'slumming parties!'[49]"

Charles Dickens visited New York in 1841, commenting that he had previously thought no slum in America could match those of London, but concluded that Five Points was a match. By the 1840's and 1850's the streets of Five Points were full of vendors, "Punch and Judy shows" (the first in the U.S.), street jugglers, fire eaters, sword swallowers, tumblers, jugglers, plate spinners, and bagpipe players.

Five Points had managed an artistic transformation into a multicultural entertainment zone.

The tenements were so crowded and the air inside so putrid, that the tenants enjoyed taking to the streets and bars in the evenings, and there was clearly no incentive to leave early. By 1851, there were 250 saloons in 22 blocks. Saloons had become an escape hatch for the pressures of life in the tenements, and alcohol was the fuel of choice to enable coping with the environment. Gambling was also a favorite way to spend the evening, and Faro was the preferred game of chance, as well as dancing in the local dancing halls.

By 1852, when the Leavys arrived, public pressure had pushed a movement to reduce crime and vice in Five Points, which by 1860, had gradually brought the area's social problems in line with other working-class neighborhoods.

The Irish men found jobs as laborers in slaughterhouses and in shipbuilding on the docks. Some went into shoemaking and tailoring. About 25% of the Irish women quickly made their way into domestic service, and most were able to "live in" and receive free room and board, which removed them from the tenements. About 50% of the women worked in the needle and sewing trades. Both groups sent every extra dollar back to families in Ireland. Between 1845 and 1865, the Irish sent $120 million dollars to Ireland, with the lion's share coming from the domestic workers.

Even though most Irish were getting some work, the discrimination against them was significant. For instance, in 1853, an advertisement in the New York Sun read:

> "WOMAN WANTED – to do general housework; she must be clean, neat, and industrious, and above all good tempered and willing. English, Scotch, Welsh, German, or any country or color will answer except Irish[50]."

This was the environment that Thomas Leavy and his two boys encountered in May 1852 as they docked in New York. Thomas might have gained work on the docks or in a slaughterhouse, and son James would have been old enough to sweep streets, but life undoubtedly could not have been much better than that.

Leavy Searches For Gold

The California gold rush began in 1848, causing the entire world's population to be green with envy and dreaming of gold. This bonanza lasted until 1855, at which time it became a "borrasca," meaning the gold had disappeared. Three hundred thousand people had rushed to California during this period, and they came from all parts of the globe — a limited number were Americans coming from the east coast.

In 1860, the travel routes from Five Points, New York to San Francisco were as follows:

1. <u>Steamship and Railroad</u> — New York or New Orleans via steam ship to Chagres, Panama; Panama railroad 48 miles across the Isthmus of Panama; then steam ship to San Francisco, a journey of 25 to 30 days duration.
2. <u>Wagon Train</u> — across the California/Oregon Trail traveling for approximately four months.
3. <u>Butterfield Stage Line</u> (1858-1861) — St. Louis to Santa Fe; San Diego; San Francisco. A 24-day trip.

Option #1 would require money for passage unless you worked on the ship. Option #2, a young man might be able to work his way across the U.S. on the wagon train.

All we know is that James H. Leavy, a teenager, left his father and brother in New York, to spread his wings by moving west to the gold fields of California. There is no evidence suggesting that his father and brother also left. Most boys during this period were considered emancipated by age 15 and would leave the home nest to strike out on their own.

Leavy's surname was spelled two different ways by historians. Initially, it appeared on the ship's manifest as Levy, and was interpreted to be a Jewish name, which stuck. James Leavy travelled into history as a famous Jewish gunfighter; however, historian Erik J. Wright, has confirmed that this was a mistake. This often happened with ship's manifests — the scribes who recorded the names of passengers were writing what they heard and were not concerned with the accuracy of their spelling. It was not an important element of record keeping during that time.

Through letters and documents signed by Leavy, the name was determined to be Leavy, and James was undoubtedly Catholic. This was confirmed by historian, Erik Wright, in his article for the *Wild West Magazine* (Feb. 2015.) Leavy is a derivation of Dunleavy, coming from the Gaelic. He may have adopted the Jewish moniker after arriving in America, thinking that he would endure less discrimination than with an Irish surname. The Irish, for the most part, were detested in New York, and jobs were often denied to anyone with an Irish heritage. Many young Irish left New York as soon as they could for hopeful opportunities in the West.

In the late 1860's, when the large silver deposit was discovered in Pioche, word travelled fast to the gold fields in California, as the placer gold (gold found in the rivers) was being depleted, forcing miners to look for the next strike. James Leavy was one of these miners, and he quickly found his way to eastern Nevada, hoping to get in on the ground floor of a new bonanza.

Miners carried guns in California, but the era of professional gunmen developed in Nevada and other neighboring states. The gold and silver deposits discovered in Nevada were underground, which resulted in a rampant epidemic of claim jumping. It's possible that Leavy developed his gun handling skills from the famous Pioche gunfighter, Morgan Courtney, who had already honed the skills and taken the persona of a professional gunfighter, becoming the "Chief" of Pioche. They were walking the same streets, drinking, and gambling in the same saloons during the early years in Pioche, and undoubtedly knew each other.

Gunfire 1,000 Feet Below

We know that James Leavy was still working in Pioche in December of 1872. The miners had become disgruntled with the Raymond and Ely management who had decided to replace the eight-hour shift with a ten-hour shift — same wages. The eight-hour shift had been established by the Comstock management in Virginia City in 1866, so the lengthening of hours underground was a significant blow and loss of autonomy for the miners. On Thursday, December 26, 1872, the day shift demanded to be hoisted to the top after eight hours; and the night shift refused to go to work. Meetings regarding unionization had ensued.

On Friday, many striking miners had already been replaced. At the same time, two Pioche mines, the Lightner and the Phoenix, had shafts or tunnels which were close to converging. The two superintendents had agreed to cease activity in that zone until agreements could be codified.

However, some Phoenix miners had connected to the Lightner drift (tunnel) and had erected a barricade. Raymond and Ely had hired a few gunfighters due to the impending strike and instructed them to build their own barricade. Of course, gunfire broke out! Miner, Thomas Ryan, at some point raised his head over the Phoenix barricade and was killed instantly by a bullet piercing his face. No one could be certain who fired the shot, but since James Leavy was the leader of the Raymond and Ely forces, suspicion fell on him.

Leavy was justifiably frightened that the Lightner miners were turning into a vigilante mob. They had just lost one of their coworkers, and underground coworkers were part of a brotherhood. Therefore, Leavy, frightened of the mob, immediately left town on foot, walking west towards Hamilton. It was the middle of winter, and his feet became frostbitten. Officials acted on a tip and were able to apprehend him on the road and bring him back to Pioche where he was jailed again. However, he was soon moved to the hospital for treatment of his feet. Ultimately amputation of several toes became necessary, with Dr. Bishop performing the surgery.

The grand jury did not indict James Leavy — maybe not enough evidence, and/or no witnesses who could be relied upon. Either way, among the fightin' men, Leavy was seen to have shot his second man, and his reputation as a gunfighter was expanding by the day. However, in spite of his growing reputation, Leavy continued to claim that he was not the shooter that killed Ryan, and he continued to sport righteous indignation about being labeled as the gunman. He finally wrote a scathing letter to the editor of the Pioche Record proclaiming his innocence:

> "In your issue of the 2nd instant I see mention of the accidental discharge of a gun in the hand of Michael Cody, and as Mr. Cody was then in search of me to kill me, I feel called upon to make a full explanation to the public. Cody's action grew out of the killing

of Ryan in the Pioche Phoenix, December 28, 1872. The report was circulated that I killed Ryan and every effort was made to influence his friends to the highest pitch against me by men who could not possibly know who did the killing. In a short time the friends of Ryan were ready to lynch me without Judge or Jury. I knew I was innocent, but I thought it best to leave until the irresponsible mob could have time to cool down. I did so, with a full sense of the injury the leaders of that mob had done me. In my journey I had my feet badly frozen and have been confined to a bed of suffering every since. Until about the 15th of last month. On the 1st of this month, I walked out and met men who had led the mob in search of me, and as they appeared to be looking at me in a very prying and unpleasant manner, a sense of the injury they had caused me aroused my highest indignation, and I gave vent of my feelings in a very earnest way, when some of them, I understand went to arm themselves and tell Cody I was on the rampage and threatening his life. Cody therefore took a double-barreled shot gun and started out with the full intention of killing me on sight, when his gun was accidentally discharged, and he was temporarily arrested. Now, I understand Cody has a number of affidavits stating that I threatened to kill him. Affidavits are getting to be very cheap and unreliable in this camp, if he has such, I hereby brand any statement to the effect that I ever, in any way, threatened

the life of Michael Cody, as a lie. I never had anything against him, and never intended to hurt him, or anybody else, if they will let me alone. As to the killing of Thomas Ryan I am as innocent as the babe unborn. I have been greatly injured by the publicity in all the papers of the land of my killing Ryan and when I think of the falsity of it, and those who so unjustly started the report, and all the suffering I have endured, I cannot be chafed in public by them without showing them that I am not so lost to manhood as not to resent it. James Leavy. Pioche April 7, 1873."
Pioche Daily Record April 10, 1873.

Leavy Becomes A "Fightin' Man"

By the end of 1873, the silver strike in Pioche was starting to play out. Morgan Courtney, Leavy's mentor had been killed; and it was time for James Leavy to move on. He spent several years in Virginia City, and by 1876, was headed to Deadwood City in the Black Hills of South Dakota, the next gold bonanza.

> A newspaper reporter in Deadwood wrote, "Every man in Deadwood carries about fourteen pounds of firearms hitched to his belt, and they never pass any words. The fellow that gets his gun out first is the best man, and they lug off the other fellow's body.... They don't kill him for what he has done, but for what he is liable to do."[51]

James Butler "Wild Bill" Hickok was living in Deadwood at this time, and was assassinated August 2, 1876, by Jack Mc Call who shot him in the back of his head. (He was ambushed as were most of the notorious gunmen.) Hickok was the most famous of the gunmen, but local pioneer, Ellis T. "Doc" Pierce also honors Jim Leavy, John Bull, Billy Allen, Tom Harwich, and Joel Collins with this propitious designation.

In March 1877, Leavy relocated to Cheyenne, Wyoming, as a resident gambler. The Cheyenne saloon crowd also included Wyatt Earp, John H. "Doc" Holliday and W.B. "Bat" Masterson. Jim

Leavy had become known as a heavy gambler in the fast-moving mining towns of Pioche, Deadwood and Cheyenne. On March 9, 1877, he became locked in a heavy argument over a game of cards with Charlie Harrison in the Shingle & Locke Saloon in Cheyenne. Bat Masterson described Charlie Harrison in his article *"Ben Thompson and other noted Gunmen,"* 1907:

> "Charlie Harrison was one of the best-known sporting men west of the Missouri River. His home was in St. Louis, but he traveled extensively throughout the West and was well-known through the Rocky Mountain region. He was of an impetuous temperament, quick of action, of unquestioned courage, and the most expert man I ever saw with a pistol. He could shoot faster and straighter when shooting at a target than any man I ever knew; then add to that the fact that no man possessed more courage than he did, and the natural conclusion would be that he would be a most formidable foe to encounter in a pistol duel[52]."

> "…It looked like 100 to 1 that Harrison would win the fight because of his well-known courage and proficiency in pistol use. Little being known at that time about Jim Levy [sic], Harrison was made a hot favorite in the betting in the various gambling resorts of Cheyenne. The men were not long in getting together after securing their revolvers, which were of the Colt's pattern and of 45-caliber in size."

"They met on opposite sides of the city's principal street and opened fire on each other without a moment's delay. Harrison, as was expected, fairly set his pistol on fire; he was shooting so fast and managed to fire five shots at Levy before the latter could draw a bead on him. Levy finally let go a shot. It was all that was necessary. Harrison tumbled into the street in a dying condition and was soon afterward laid to rest alongside of others who had gone before in a similar way."[53]

After a shootout with such a noted gunfighter as Charlie Harrison, James Leavy was now famous throughout the West for his gun handling abilities. Together the men had fired seven shots — one of Leavy's rounds struck Harrison in the breast and wounded him. Leavy ran up to Harrison and shot him again in the lower abdomen. He died a week later. After standing trial for murder, Leavy was acquitted. Oh, the luck of the Irish!

"John "Crooked Mouth" Green, who was described by William Pinkerton as a notorious Chicago crook, testified under oath about Leavy, the victor in the duel, "I have known him by reputation for 10 years…Cheyenne, Deadwood and different places." Green said, when asked if Leavy's reputation had been for peace and quietness or the reverse, Green responded, 'His reputation has always been that of a very dangerous man. A man that would kill a man without the least provocations, a desperate man, and a desperado.'" Green added that Leavy's reputation had spread as far as Chicago and St. Louis.[54]"

By June 1877, Leavy was in Leadville, Colorado, and by 1880, he had traveled south to Tombstone, Arizona, a newly established Mexican border town. Of course, being an avid Faro player, he soon met up again with his old friends, Wyatt Earp, and Doc Holliday — gambling men of the first order.

As fate would have it, David Neagle, the man who shot and disfigured Leavy, was also in Tombstone, but evidently the two were able to give each other a nod and move on. I doubt that either man wished to go head-to-head with the other — they were too well matched.

Leavy was also reunited with two of his old gambling friends, Charley Storms, and Dublin Trix (also known as Dublin Lyons), the two gentlemen who posted bail for him in Cheyenne, and who were known for their cheating habits when gambling. However, this twosome met their match when Storms was shot outside the Oriental Saloon by a friend of Wyatt Earp, and when Earp quickly ordered Lyons to leave town —Lyons knew that any challenge to the Earp brothers was suicide.

That same month, February 1881, Jim Leavy staked water rights claims at three locations with partners, Richard "Dick" Clark, Wyatt Earp, and Doc Holliday. The latter three were partners in the famous Oriental Saloon. The western historian, Gary Roberts, alleges that in 1881, Leavy was, by far, the best known of the four water rights' partners.

New Friends: The Earp's & Holliday

By Spring of 1882, Leavy made his way 70 miles northwest to Tucson. On June 5th, it's reported that he entered the Fashion Saloon on West Congress Street — drunk and sporting an entourage. William Moyer was dealing that day at John Murphy's Faro table.

> "After losing heavily for a time at the Murphy Faro table, Leavy proclaimed, "The game is foul," and continued to argue with the dealer and the owner — Moyer and Murphy. An eyewitness, William Gale, later testified that Leavy called the two out saying, "You have been making a talking fight. Now you've got to fight.[55]"

Author, David Grasse, reports that Leavy made repeated threats to Moyer and Murphy promising, "to waltz on their layout and shoot their checks from the table," and further that, "he was going to the Mexican line and they would fight across the wagon track." Also, Grasse states that Leavy borrowed $50 from Matt Reading of the El Dorado saloon to buy a pistol and hire a wagon team to drive the group to the border the next morning for the duel. He said he would, "Make the sons of bitches fight or he would kill them all.[56]"

Leavy's reputation had proceeded him. John Murphy, owner of the Faro game, after analyzing his odds, reckoned that a duel was not at all advisable; wherein, he concocted a plan to ambush Leavy. He calculated that with Leavy's serious drinking, his impetuous nature, and his sure "dead eye" reputation with a gun, that it was surely Leavy's life or his at this point.

Historian Erick Wright reports in an article for the *Wild West Magazine* that:

> "At about 10 p.m. Leavy was walking with gambling friend George Duncan toward the Palace Hotel on South Meyer Street. As Leavy approached the hotel entrance, several shots rang out nearly simultaneously. Despite the overhead gaslights, hotel clerk, William Hopkins, could only make out the flashes of the guns and not the faces of the shooters." Dr. Dexter Lyford later testified that Leavy dropped beneath an awning near a bootblack stand across the street from the hotel. He had been shot five times—like his Pioche mentor, Courtney—with all but one of the bullet wounds being potentially fatal.[57]"

> According to Lyford, "Leavy had entry wounds on the right and left side of his neck just above the collarbone; each ball had traced its way down Leavy's spinal column and lodged in his vertebrae. The third wound Lyford described came from a ball that had entered Leavy's right side, near the sixth or seventh rib, and traced upward, lodging in the heart. The fourth wound was in Leavy's right arm above the elbow, with the ball exiting below the entrance wound. The final wound, and perhaps the most grotesque, was from a

ball that had passed through Leavy's upper lip, lodging in the soft bone between the eyes. The trajectories of the latter two balls suggest Leavy had been shot again when already down."[58]

Witnesses who ran to the scene immediately after the shooting, heard Murphy, Moyer and their gambler friend, Dave Gibson, each take credit for the shooting of Leavy. A newspaper reporter from the *Arizona Daily Star* was among the throng that was gathering around Leavy where he was lying on the street gasping for last breath, and he observed that no weapon was evident on his person. Riddled with bullets, James Leavy's last words were, "My God. Has it come to this?[59]"

Hugh Farley was the prosecutor at the preliminary hearing on June 8th, and the three assailants were represented by Tom Fitch, the defense attorney who had represented Wyatt Earp three months prior during his trial regarding the vendetta ride he took rounding up the "Cowboys," a gang of renegades who had terrorized the town of Tombstone and who had ambushed his brothers, Virgil and Morgan Earp at the O.K. Corral.

> The attorneys in the Murphy/ Moyer matter "elicited testimony from 42 witnesses, including miner Tom Langley, who heard one of the trio declare, 'Here is our game!' as they raised their six-shooters at Leavy." And, Langley continued, "After Levy [sic] fell, Gibson walked to where he lay and shot in the direction where he lay.[60]"

The Judge ruled that there was probable cause to send the three to a grand jury; however, the co-defendants must have been very skeptical of standing trial, as on October 23, 1882, they successfully managed an escape from the Pima County Jail. You could probably call it a successful jail break because William Moyer was not apprehended again until July 1883 — at a gambling hall in Denver! Moyer was tried and again defended by Tom Fitch but was found guilty and sentenced to 99 years in Yuma Territorial Prison. He was pardoned in 1888 — just five years later!

Murphy and Gibson were apprehended at about the same time in the mining camp of Fenner, California, near San Bernardino. The pair had adopted aliases, and Gibson was driving a stagecoach route. Murphy was tried first in 1884, where he testified that he too was born in Ireland. He was acquitted. Gibson was tried in early 1884, as well, and was also acquitted.

Oh, the luck of the Irish!

> "Murphy lived his life as a gambler in southern Arizona and is buried in Tucson. Gibson continued to work in mining and prospecting and died in Prescott, Arizona. Moyer, however, worked at periods as a hired gun and was involved in the Johnnie Mine fight in Nevada in 1895. He was last seen in Alaska around the turn of the twentieth century.[61]"

George Duncan, who said he had known Levy for seven or eight years in Virginia City, Cheyenne, Deadwood, and Tucson, stated that shortly before the shooting, Levy had told him he did not have a friend in the world and that he couldn't find anyone to second him in the duel. He didn't even have a gun, and tried to borrow Duncan's but was refused. The witness said he saw Murphy fire the first two shots and Gibson fire two more. When the shooting began, he said he heard Levy cry out, "My God! Don't murder me, I'm not armed.[62]"

Outnumbered And Outgunned

Jim Leavy seemed to have been forgotten after his
death, in spite of being hailed by his peers, Bat
Masterson and Wyatt Earp, as one of the most
notorious gunfighters of his time. He died as he
lived, by the gun, but at the end he was ambushed, as
no one dared to take him on face to face, which was
the case of most of the fastest gunfighters in the Wild
West.

Charles Driscoll, an acquaintance of Moyer,
submitted a character letter to the Territorial
Governor in Moyer's defense after the trial as follows:

> "I signed it gladly, knowing the facts in the
> case so well. Knowing also that if anyone
> should suffer for the killing of Levy [sic]
> Murphy is the man. I knew all the parties
> concerned intimately. Knew Murphy better
> than any of the others but had known Levy
> [sic] longer. A smooth, intelligent fellow
> when not under the influence of opium or
> liquor but had come to a stage in his career
> when someone had to kill him for the good
> and peace of the community. He had
> intimidated everyone with whom he came in
> contact. All men not fighters feared him. I
> was in Cheyenne when he killed Harrison. At
> that time, he was not an opium fiend. He
> knew enough about gambling to play at faro
> but not enough to deal the game or protect
> himself...Levy made it a point to abuse

Moyer, who was employed by Murphy as a dealer…threatening to turn the table over and making threats generally that would drive all timid players away from the game and out of the house.[63]"

There is no evidence that James Leavy during his twenty years roaming the western U.S. ever married, had children, or formed any meaningful long-term relationships. There is no mention of his father or his brother. Jim Leavy had suffered trauma as a young child, witnessing starvation deaths, surviving weeks on the high seas in a crowded, putrid "coffin ship", and then enduring the ostracization by New Yorkers due to his Irish heritage. All these things were a perfect setup for a lonely, single male to eventually find relief through substance abuse, and opium was readily available and affordable in the wild west.

The addiction may have started when he lost his toes due to frost bite in Pioche. He stated that he had been in excruciating pain for months, and opium was the most available and effective pain killer of the time. He wasn't as good a gambler as he wanted to be, and the opium addiction wouldn't have enhanced those skills either. This led to him losing his money and his gun — and, therefore, Jim Leavy was unarmed when the ambush occurred. A very sad ending to a hard life.

His passing went mostly unnoticed in Tucson, and it is only surmised that he is buried in an unmarked grave in Tucson's defunct Court Street Cemetery.

He is, however, memorialized by one admirer, old-timer, Albert Franklin Banta, who wrote forty years later about the circumstances of Leavy's death, stating that he was "Shot by cowardly assassins," and that

"Jim Levy [sic] had more 'sand' in one of his fingers than the three yellow-streaked curs had in their three bodies combined. Given even half a show (and the curs knew it,) Jim Levy would have cleaned up the three at one and the same time — if the cowardly curs had attempted to face the music. Al three were bullies or 'four flushers,' and it is a notorious fact that class of cattle are notoriously 'yellow' without a single exception.[64]"

[43] "I knew very well": Gracey, op.cit

[45]"The shooting commenced": Gracey, op.cit
[46] "Casey's friends were now enemies": Gracey op.cit
[47] "That apartments in the worst part": Tyler Anbinder, "Five Points, Free Press, Division of Simon and Shuster, 2001
[48]"The old dame of sixty": Tyler Anbinder, Ibid
[49] "The buildings are little, old": Tyler Anbinder, op. cit
[50]"Woman wanted to do": Tyler Anbinder, op.cit
[51] "Every man in Deadwood carries": Robert K DeArment, Deadly Dozen: Forgotten Gunfighters of the Old West. Volume 3, 1925
[52] "Charlie Harrison was one": Bat Masterson, "Famous Gunfighters of the Western Frontier, 2020, Digireads.
[53] "It looked like 100 to 1": Bat Masterson, Ibid
[54]"John Crooked Mouth Green": Erik Wright, Wild West Magazine, vol.27 No. 5, Feb. 2015, Weider History Group, Inc. Leesburg, Va.
[55] "After losing heavily for a time": Wright, Ibid
[56] "He was going to the Mexican line": David Grasse, "God, Has it come to this?" The killing of James Leavy and Criminal Justice in Territorial Arizona, The Journal of Arizona History. Vol 57 #2 (2016) 11-52 Accessed March 13, 2020
[57]"At about 10:00p.M., Leavy": Wright, op. cit.
[58]"Leavy had entry wounds" Wright, op.cit
[59] "My God has it come to this?": Wright, op. cit.
[60] "Here is our game!": Wright, op. cit.
[61]"Murphy lived his life": Wright, op.cit
[62] "He didn't even have a gun": De Arment, op. cit
[63] "I signed it gladly": Wright, op. cit
[64] "He is however, memorialized": Wright op. cit

Part IV David Butler Neagle

Gunfighter

The Neagles Arrive In Pioche

Early in 1870, an energetic, young couple, David B. Neagle, age 23, and Bertha Bousquet, age 17, rode into Pioche on one of the stagecoach lines from White Pine County or from Salt Lake City. David had been mining in Treasure City (White Pine County) the location of present-day Ely, Nevada. The ore in Treasure City was nearing depletion; and, thus, so was the population of the town. Most Treasure City miners were cashing in their chips and moving on to Pioche, the newest boomtown with the most promise.

It is alleged that David had met Bertha in Salt Lake City while on a trip possibly to check out jobs in that area, and she had agreed to return with him to Pioche. The couple entered the town presenting themselves as Mr. and Mrs. Neagle, but they were not married, and who was to know or care in Pioche?

The couple settled down in Pioche — the best way that anyone could at that time — which meant they either lived in a boarding house, or a one-room miner's cabin. Those were the only choices. The couple became parents on April 14, 1870, when Louisa was born, and the stork visited them a second time on Oct. 7, 1871, with the birth of Emma.

David was gainfully employed in one of the Pioche mines as a miner and seemed to have quickly become part of the miner's network of friends and enemies —

a network that could unravel faster than a cable knit sweater.

The Newland Mine ambush orchestrated by Morgan Courtney occurred in November of 1870. The Neagles had been in town six months or so by that time, and David had apparently already become fast friends with Mike Casey, one of the Courtney gang responsible for the ambush and death of Mr. Gorson. This becomes apparent because in June 1871, David participated in what appeared to be an ambush of James Leavy, an avowed enemy of Casey.

Casey had called Leavy out on Main Street that warm June day, because Leavy had testified in court against Casey, saying that Casey fired the first shot at Gorson. Leavy went home to retrieve his gun, preparing for a one-on-one gunfight with Casey. He returned through an alley in order to get the advantage of surprise. He called out to Casey and then fired, grazing his skull. Casey dove at Leavy; Leavy fired again striking him in the neck, and then struck Casey in the head with the blunt end of his pistol — the final death blow.

David Neagle had been waiting in front of Freudenthal's store, obviously intending to back up Casey, but when Leavy intercepted Casey from the alley, Neagle ran into the street, pulled his gun with his left hand, and took several shots at Leavy hitting him in the lower jaw. Casey was dead, and Leavy was now wounded. The sheriff apprehended both Leavy and Neagle and threw them into the same cell. Leavy was badly hurt and took several months to recover — his cheek and mouth were scarred due to Neagle's bullet which left him with a sinister look from that time forward. The grand jury quickly discharged David Neagle, as was common in Pioche.

The Next Mine Will Be Better

After several years of successful mining in Pioche, history repeated itself, and the rich ore veins gradually began to disappear into the clay earth — one by one. Seeing the writing on the wall, Neagle packed up Bertha and his daughters and headed out for a new mine at Panamint City, California, located in the mountains just west of Death Valley. The family arrived June 26, 1874.

Panamint was very good for David — a place where he achieved much success. He packed in alcohol on mules and established the first saloon. He sent a letter back to Bob Archer in Pioche reporting:

> "I seldom advise parties to come to new mining camps, but in this instance, I have no hesitancy in giving you all the information you desire, and advice also. I consider this the richest mining camp on the Coast…" All of Nevada was referred to as the "coast" during the 1800's[65].

David Neagle, only 24 by that time, was very handy with a gun, as he had already interacted with the gunmen, Leavy and Casey; and undoubtedly with the "Chief of Pioche", Morgan Courtney — a fearsome trio to be sure. In fact, Neagle may have crossed paths with Courtney in Virginia City, when Morgan was still using his birth name, Richard Moriarty. David Neagle was listed in the city directory for Gold Hill, one mile downhill from Virginia City, in the years 1868 and 1869. Richard Moriarty had killed O'Toole in a Virginia City saloon on November 16, 1868. It was still a very small State with only a handful of towns, and they were all mining towns attracting the same workforce. David had to have known or at least known of Richard, as the killing of O'Toole was major news across the State. Also, Moriarty and several other of his Irish buddies lived in Gold Hill — not Virginia City. So, it seems very likely that their paths had crossed.

Irish Roots

David Butler Neagle was born October 10, 1847, in Boston, Massachusetts, to William Neagle and Bridget Donahue Neagle, both Irish immigrants. Bridget, age 15 traveling with her father, Terence Donahue, and siblings, Ann (16), Patricia (13), as well as two other teenagers, probably cousins, Margaret (17) and Catherine (15) Sheridien, had sailed on the Ship "Sapphire" from Ireland, docking on April 28, 1826.

All these young travelers were teenagers, old enough to gain employment in Boston as maids or servants in the homes of Bostonians, and to earn enough money to send most of their earnings back to their families in Ireland. The Irish families could then purchase passage for other family members. This was the favored plan for saving Irish families from starvation, and Terence Donahue was the chosen adult to accompany these five teenagers to America, the land of opportunity.

The "Neagle" family name is of Norman Irish origin. In Ireland it could be spelled Neagle or Nangle, which was an anglicized version of the original "de Angulos." This family was granted several large tracts of land in county Cork and North Connach in the 12th Century right after the Norman invasion.

The name "Donahue" was a derivation of O'Donoghue and can be traced back to ancient times in County Kerry. Bridget Donahue and William Neagle, a plasterer in Boston, were married Feb. 2,

1845. The lifestyle of Irish immigrants in Boston was much the same as in New York City. The first immigrants into Boston in the 1820's, were Protestant, who were accepted quite well by the Protestant Yankees; but as more Catholic Irish arrived, things changed dramatically.

The Irish initially settled in East Boston on the streets close to the docks where most of the men would get jobs. As in New York, the Irish Catholics were hired as workers and servants, but there was little social interaction between the new immigrants and the Protestant natives. In fact, the immigrants were seen as both a spiritual and a political threat and were often bullied by roving bands of Protestants who would damage their property and strike fear into the newly arrived Irish.

Many of the immigrants were weakened by typhus when they arrived in the coffin ships and were quarantined on Deer Island, where large numbers lost their lives. Then, to add to the misery of the new citizens, a cholera epidemic swept through Boston in 1849, as it had in New York. The poor immigrants were living in unsanitary conditions on the waterfront and were hit the worst — over 500 Irish died.

Boston health inspectors described a typical Irish slum as a "Perfect hive of human beings without comforts and mostly without common necessities, in many cases huddled together like brutes, without regard to age, or sex, or sense of decency.[66]"

In the 1840's and 50's, the protestant backed political party in power passed laws barring Irish Catholics from burial in public cemeteries; requiring children to read from King James (Protestant version) of the Bible and sing Protestant hymns, etc.

Governor Gardner, the Massachusetts Governor, in an 1855 speech, stated:

> "During the present decade, nearly four millions of aliens will probably be poured upon us...nearly four-fifths of the beggary, two-thirds of the pauperism, and more than three-fifths of the crimes spring from our foreign population."

> In 1856, he again spoke, "They should have the entire regulation of the admission and transfer of paupers to the different Almshouses, — of removing the alien pauper insane to the Lunatic Hospitals, — of sending paupers out of the state to those places where they have a settlement...[67]"

Fortunately, this was Gardner's final term as Governor.

It's no wonder that many Irish, hearing about the riches being made in the West, sought to move their families. William and Bridget shared these dreams and left Boston in 1852, with David (age 5), and his sister, Mary (age 6), to settle in San Francisco.

As with James Leavy, it is unknown how they got there, by land on a wagon train, or by sea across the Isthmus of Panama, or around the southern horn on a clipper ship. We simply know that the family arrived and settled in the Mission District of San Francisco, and that, unfortunately, Bridget died shortly after.

William Neagle was committed to raising young David on his own but made the decision to place his young daughter in the city's "Female Orphan Asylum." California was a tough environment, requiring tough decisions for many.

Young David was placed in a Roman Catholic school at Santa Clara when he was ten years of age. This school eventually became Santa Clara College. However, in 1862, by age 15 (the accepted age of emancipation during that time), young David took off for one of the roughest mining camps in the West — Florence, in the Idaho Territory — in search of gold. This mining claim, located in the northwestern part of the territory, is a very remote and unnavigable area. In fact, even today it would take a four-wheel drive to get there. It's very likely that David became acquainted with guns while in Idaho, a virtually lawless territory at this time. This is about the same time (1862 – 63) that Richard Moriarty arrived from British Columbia to join the placer gold miners at the creeks of the Boise Basin.

In 1863, David's father, William, died, and David returned to San Francisco, presumably for the funeral and to handle the estate. He also returned to Santa Clara to finish his schooling, which must have looked much more appealing after his experiences in the Idaho Territory.

We next find evidence of David in Virginia City and Gold Hill (Nevada) in 1868-69 where he resumed his interest in gold mining.

Bertha was born at sea in 1853, on route from France to the U.S., and was given the name of Bertha

Blanche Bousquet. Her mother was Melenie
Bousquet or Brusque, a Basque name. Her father did
not travel with them, and I was unable to determine
his identity. I don't know if Melenie and infant,
Bertha, landed in Boston or New York, but they
found their way to San Francisco, where, presumably,
Bertha was raised.

Neagle Becomes Saloon Owner

After the four years spent in Pioche, the young Neagles arrived in Panamint, California, where David quickly went to work establishing the first saloon. "He pitched a tent, set up a board across two whisky [sic] barrels, and declared the Oriental Saloon open for business." .... "The saloon prospered and eventually the tent was replaced with a frame building, twenty by fifty feet, $10,000 worth of fixtures, a billiard table, a black walnut bar, Inyo pine wainscotings finished to look like oak, a number of paintings of nude females, and two gambling rooms[68]."

Oh, did I mention that the walls of the saloon were lined with corrugated iron to protect the customers from flying bullets—of course, Panamint was a wild-cat mining town!

The saloon soon became the center for social and political meetings. Religious services were also conducted there, as well as theatrical plays. David Neagle, now a very proud businessman was maturing with this success. He purchased an entire block of real estate on the main street and proceeded to subdivide and sell lots for a handsome profit.

In 1874, David and Bertha were married; David registered to vote in Inyo County, California, and on August 1, 1875, Bertha gave birth to a third daughter, Winifred, called Winnie by her parents.

227

However, not all was roses in Panamint, as the couple suffered the heartbreaking deaths of their two older daughters, Louisa on February 15, 1875, and Emma, October 21, 1876. I was unable to find cause of death for either daughter, but the Neagles were left mourning, and now with only one child, Winnie.

Meanwhile, David entered politics, trying to affect the removal of the Panamint mining district from the County of Inyo, and the moving of the County seat to Panamint. He also made an unsuccessful run for County Recorder.

However, in late 1875, a trifecta of unfortunate economic calamities occurred. Due to a national bank panic, mining stocks dropped dramatically; the proposed railroad connecting Surprise Canyon, the location of Panamint, to a larger railroad line, was scuttled; and the rich Panamint ore was disappearing at an alarming rate.

The eventual exodus from Panamint began, and once again the Neagles packed up and moved out — reportedly, leaving with about $20,000 ($440,000 today.) They moved back to Virginia City, which was not too far away, and they reunited with David's sister, Mary, who had successfully graduated from the girl's asylum, had married, and was now living in Virginia City. It was reported that Neagle opened a bar while there called the "Capital," but I was not able to confirm any such bar.

Miners Must Travel

Once the Neagle's left Virginia City for the second time, it appears that David was hell-bent on striking it rich by discovering a new ore strike of his own, and the family embarked on a new, but equally different wild ride.

They first traveled to Prescott, Arizona, where David took a job as a mine foreman, but was continuously prospecting for his own claim, as well. *The Prescott Weekly Mine,* reported in July 1877, that "Dave Nagle [sic] a good prospector and miner is sinking a shaft on the Goodwin and is now down about 50 feet and considers the ore fair and his prospect flattering[69]."

Evidently that body of ore did not "pan out," as David was reported to be working a gold claim on Turkey Creek when he fell and injured one leg, which became infected. He almost lost the leg but was able to recover after four months of bed rest.

He then traveled to Bodie, California, to mine when the infection in his leg returned with a vengeance, and he was forced to return to San Francisco. After recovering a second time, Neagle quickly resumed his energetic search for the next gold bonanza traveling to Utah, where he mined for silver at the Horn Silver Mining Company; to the headwaters of the Snake River in Wyoming (placer mining;) to various Arizona mines; and to Sonora, Mexico where he was foreman of a mine. It's not clear which of these ventures included Bertha and Winnie.

It makes my head spin and my bones ache to think of the long days traveling by stage, railroad, or horse cart between these locations — some of which are hundreds of miles apart. Evidently the mine at Sonora had shut down, and David had to seriously consider his friend Cochise County Arizona sheriff John H. Behan's offer of a job as a deputy. The two men had known each other since 1877, in Prescott. These rolling stone types of men were bound to cross one another's path frequently, as they were all circling through the same western mining camps. (This continued for another 100 years, as my grandfather worked at many of the same places during his mining years in the early 1900's – including Wyoming, Mexico, Arizona, and Nevada.)

Politics In Tombstone

David Neagle and John Behan had known each other in Prescott, they were both of Irish American descent, and both were interested in politics. Behan moved to Tombstone on September 14, 1880, with his son, Albert, and with his fiancé, nineteen-year-old Josephine Marcus, a sometimes bar girl/sometimes aspiring actress. David, Bertha, and Winnie had arrived several months before on July 15, 1880.

The County of Cochise had just been formed with Tombstone as the County seat. John C. Fremont had appointed officers until official elections scheduled for November 1882 could be held. Three of the Earp brothers had also just arrived in Tombstone — Wyatt, Virgil, and Morgan, along with Doc Holliday.

Wyatt was a Republican and fully expected the Republican Governor would appoint him as tax collector and sheriff. Unfortunately, for Wyatt, Behan had powerful Democratic friends who were successful in getting him appointed to both offices.

Wyatt did not take this slight well, which fueled a major feud between the two; and the fire got hotter when Wyatt made it known that he was waiting in the wings if the relationship between Behan and Josephine Marcus faltered.

Behan appointed David Neagle as a deputy, and the Earp brothers went to work for Wells Fargo as stagecoach messengers (guards.) As time went on, David became friends with the Earps and became somewhat disenchanted with John Behan's political dealings, which were always tipped against the Earps. David was walking a fine line between the two factions.

One of Behan's loyal followers, Billy Breakenridge said this of Neagle, "Nagel [sic] was very much in evidence in Tombstone in the early eighties…He was a fearless officer and a good one[70]."

Fred Dodge, an Earp supporter described Neagle as a "Square man (who) could not tolerate the work of Johnny Behan and there was a sure and final break between the two.[71]"

In 1881, Neagle, a very busy and efficient law officer, made notable collars. In September 1881, he arrested fellow deputies, Frank Stitwell and Pete Spence on suspicion of stagecoach robbery. In July 1881, David also arrested Doc Holliday on suspicion of stagecoach robbery. In November 1881, he arrested John Ringo, charged with robbery of a poker game. And, in January 1882, Sherman McMaster (gunfighter for Wyatt Earp) was arrested for discharging a pistol in the Oriental Saloon.

Each of these arrests was made by Neagle, a man 5' 7" tall and 145 lbs., without the use of deadly force.

Luckily, David Neagle was out of town on business at the time of the O.K. Corral shoot out, which occurred between the Earp brothers and Doc Holliday against the Clanton and Mc Lawry cowboys.

On December 28, 1881, David Neagle was elected as City Marshal and in short order he appointed Irishmen, James Kenny, James Coyle, Harry Salon, and Joseph Poynton as deputies — Clan first and foremost!

During the early morning of May 10, 1882, a group of Mexican nationals were celebrating Cinco de Mayo—a continuation of the night before—and were discharging weapons in front of a saloon in the Mexican quarter. Deputy Joe Poynton was called to quell the disturbance. He arrested two men who where arraigned, fined, and allowed to return to their friends in order to raise money for the fines. Poynton escorted the two back to the saloon, but after being threatened, he returned the prisoners to the jail and started searching for his boss, Neagle.

Poynton and Neagle decided to return together to the saloon, intending to disarm and arrest the troublemakers. When they arrived, Figueroa, one of the revelers, took out a Henry rifle, shot Poynton and started running. Neagle returned the shot but failed to hit the assailant. He returned to his office to retrieve his Winchester rifle, commandeered a horse, and took off after Figueroa who was presumably still on foot. He caught up to him in about half-a-mile and shouted to him to stop — Figueroa kept running. Neagle shot twice and killed the man with the second shot.

The coroner's jury exonerated Neagle of any blame. With a good record as a deputy, he was now in a secure position to run against John Behan for sheriff. Disgusted with the infighting of the Democrats, Neagle ran as an Independent, but only succeeded in dividing the Democratic vote, ending up being defeated by Jerome Ward.

David Neagle then proceeded to prove himself to be as poor a loser as Wyatt Earp, accusing Milt Joyce, a county supervisor, of working against him — accosting the man and beating him up. After that, David realized he had ruined any chance of further political aspirations in Tombstone and moved his family back to Prescott. His son, Albert, was born in Prescott in 1883.

In short, David Neagle had proven to be a mixed bag. During the election he had very strong support of the miners in the area, and some felt he was responsible for driving Wyatt Earp and his gunmen out of town. Fred Dodge noted, "he was a fast gun and that only (Bat) Masterson and (Johnny) Ringo might be in his class.[72]"

However, the *Epitaph,* newspaper editor had a different take on Neagle, "his hasty ungovernable temper, his inclination to harsh measures, his habit of drawing and using firearms to intimidate when unwarranted by facts, all prove him to be an unfit person to trust…. the office of sheriff.[73]"

Let's Try Montana

By early 1884, David Neagle, who was always ready to travel and a firm believer in new beginnings, had transported his family, now including the infant, Albert, to Montana. He negotiated a contract to provide newly cut lumber to the Anaconda Company which was operating near Butte, Montana. Unfortunately, On March 1, his business partner, Maginnis, absconded with $600 from the newly formed company — money which was earmarked for payroll.

Neagle, who appeared to be very competent as a rider, as well as with weapons, pursued the man on horseback, and took down the thief with one bullet. The man lingered several days, but eventually died from the wound. In a preliminary hearing, Neagle was exonerated and became a hero at the woodcutter's camp for recovering the payroll; however, as before, not everyone agreed with his method of vigilante justice.

Late in 1885, the Neagles were on the move again back to San Francisco. There, he once again aligned himself politically and received appointments to State jobs: sergeant of arms at the State legislature, deputy sheriff assigned to the license bureau, and special deputy marshal to maintain order at the polls, where he was generally assigned to polls in rough areas. His reputation had preceded him.

Within the next two years, David Neagle found himself taking a major role in a California legal dispute which played out like a melodrama turning into a Greek tragedy. Due to the myriad of colorful characters in this convoluted series of events, I will present each character separately along with his or her recent background in order to set the stage for this drama.

"The Tale Of Two Davids"

The Characters:

<u>David Neagle</u>—We know a lot about David by this point — fastest gun in town; family man; likes politics and aligns himself with powerful political leaders wherever he goes — likes to be on the right side of the law, but most always reverts to "wild west" remedies, taking the law into his own hands.

<u>William Sharon</u>—Millionaire; President of the Bank of California, the main bank handling the wealth derived from the Comstock Lode discovery in Virginia City, Nevada; recently elected Senator from Nevada; widower; now age 60; recently taking a mistress, Sarah Althea Hill, when he was supporting in a grand manner at a posh San Francisco hotel.

<u>David Terry</u>—Born 1823 in Kentucky; fought under Sam Houston and became an early Texas Ranger, serving as a Lieutenant in the Mexican War; joined the rush to California in 1849 in search of gold; practiced law for 20 years, gaining respect as a foremost legal mind in the State. He also served as Chief Justice of the California Supreme Court; he resigned that position to fight a duel with U.S. Senator David Broderick — killing Broderick over the issue of slavery (he was pro slavery) and was indicted for murder after the duel — but was acquitted (the grand jury felt that killing a man in the course of a duel was not murder — only a fair fight). He always carried a bowie knife and had stabbed a

man in the lobby of the Mark Hopkins Hotel; known for a bad temper!

<u>Stephen J. Field</u>—Justice of the U.S. Supreme Court (California was a part of Judge Field's territory and the justices of the Supreme Court traveled a circuit at this time and often filled in for other justices when needed). Field took Terry's place on the Supreme Court when Terry resigned to participate in the duel, risking his own death while defending the institution of slavery; Justice Field and David Terry did not agree on politics and were adversarial.

<u>Sarah Althea Hill</u>—The girl! — Resident of San Francisco; attractive and buxom; had worked as a prostitute in a brothel; became the mistress of William Sharon; was kept by him in a stylish suite of hotel rooms; and provided with a monthly allowance of $500 (about $11,000 today.)

Act I

<u>Scene 1</u> — William Sharon tires of Sarah Althea Hill, who was often overly dramatic and prone to violent and unhinged actions. He tries to end the relationship, but Sarah (who usually goes by Althea,) refuses to leave the hotel. Sharon evicts her by ripping out the carpets, removing door hinges, and writing a check for $7,500 ($165,000 today.) He then begins a new relationship — Althea sees red and sues him for adultery — but were they married?

<u>Scene 2</u>—David Terry, now a practicing attorney after the duel, takes Althea's case as her attorney and produces a marriage certificate as evidence of a valid

marriage to Sharon. Sharon countersues, alleging that the marriage contract was fraudulent.

Scene 3—Justice Fields, assigned to the California Circuit Court, would hear the case of Sharon v. Sharon. William Sharon dies November 13, 1885; his son and son-in-law step in on his behalf to continue defending the adultery lawsuit and pursuing the counter suit contending a fraudulent marriage contract.

Scene 4—Attorney Terry and his now girlfriend, Althea, then produce a handwritten will that Althea says she found in Sharon's desk which awarded his entire estate to her, opening a second legal case. David Terry and Althea are married January 7, 1886, in Stockton, California.

Act II

Scene 1—January 1886, two U.S. circuit judges' rule that the marriage contract was a forgery. The newly married couple are sent to jail when they refuse to turn the forged marriage document over to the court. In March 1888, they return to the court demanding further relief, where oral arguments were heard by Justices Field, Sawyer, and Sabin, who agree to take the case under advisement.

Scene 2—On August 14, 1888, Judge Sawyer encountered the couple on a train between Fresno and Sacramento, where Mrs. Terry (Althea) insults Sawyer, pulls his hair, and threatens him. In September 1888, Judge Fields delivers the final opinion on the Sharon will, ruling the will a forgery. Althea screams obscenities in the courtroom and tries to pull her revolver from her handbag. Her husband and attorney, David Terry, draws his Bowie knife and hits Marshall Frank, knocking out a tooth. Althea's handbag proves to be secreting an English Bulldog pistol with five loaded chambers.

 Scene 3 — One of the peacekeepers in the courtroom that day was Deputy Marshal David Neagle, who had no official status, but was just sitting in. As the action unfolded, Neagle jumped in and grabbed Terry, assisting in holding the very large man down.

> "When he was finally allowed to stand up, Terry slid a hand inside his vest, pulled out a knife, and raised it over his head. Neagle said he heard him repeatedly threaten to 'carve his way out of there'. The officers seized him again, and a deputy marshal named Taggart held a six-shooter right to his temple and told him to drop the knife. With his right hand, Neagle grabbed the knife by the blade and with his left bent Terry's fingers until Terry released his grip on the handle.[74]"

Once again, left-handed David Neagle to the rescue.

Both Terrys are arrested and sentenced for "contempt of court," with David Terry serving six months in jail and Althea one month.

Scene 4—Mr. and Mrs. Terry continue to threaten Judge Field. In July 1889, the California Supreme Court reverses themselves and rules that Althea and William Sharon were never legally married because they had kept the marriage a secret. Judge Field was scheduled to return to California again in 1890, and due to continued threats by the Terrys, Attorney General Miller instructed Marshal Frank to appoint David Neagle as a Marshal to guard and protect Judge Field.

Act III

Scene 1—On August 14, 1889, Judge Field, accompanied by Marshal David Neagle, was on a train between Los Angeles and Sacramento. As fate would have it in any good Greek tragedy, David and Althea Terry had boarded the same train! The Judge and Neagle were informed of this.

The train stopped, as scheduled, at 7:10 a.m. for breakfast at Lathrop, California. Neagle encouraged Judge Field to stay on the train and have food brought in, but Judge Field refused. Neagle was concerned about the Terrys and asked the conductor to call for the local Lathrop Constable.

Scene 2—Althea spotted Judge Field in the dining room and quickly returned to the train for her satchel and pistol. David Terry crossed the dining room behind Judge Field and proceeded to slap him from behind, knocking off his glasses and causing the Judge to stagger. Terry, of course, was 6'3" and 250 lbs. Neagle, 5'7" and 145 lbs., rose from his chair and said, "Stop that! I am an officer." Terry drew back his hand as if to maybe strike the judge again or draw his Bowie knife.

Wiry David Neagle, known by numerous accounts as one of the fastest guns in the West, drew his 45-caliber revolver with his left hand, and without one second's hesitation shot David Terry in the heart. Terry fell backwards as Neagle took a quick second shot. There were 80 to 100 people in the dining room. Neagle addressed the crowd saying, "I am a United States Marshal, and I defy anyone to touch me![75]"

Scene 3—Althea was held at the door, and a search revealed an English Bulldog pistol in her satchel. Screaming, she then rushed through the crowd and threw herself on her husband's body. Later her husband's Bowie knife was found in her satchel beside the pistol.

Act IV

Scene 1 — David Neagle and the shaken Judge Field reboard the train and lock themselves in their cabin. Althea tried to enter. Soon the Constable of Lathrop and the Stanislaus County Sheriff arrive. Neagle produces the document showing he had been appointed Marshal by the California Attorney General to protect Judge Field. However, regardless of the document, Marshal Walker arrested Neagle and took him to jail in Stockton, incarcerating him for a week. Outside, a mob of David Terry supporters milled about the streets demanding a "necktie party".

Finally, after additional attempts to keep Neagle in the Stockton jail, the U.S. attorney in San Francisco filed a writ of Habeas Corpus to release him.

Scene 2—The State of California, on behalf of Sheriff Cunningham, appealed to the U.S. Supreme Court based on whether David Neagle was acting in pursuance of the law when he shot David Terry.

242

"Justice Field testified that in his opinion, if Neagle had not shot Terry when he did, he (Field) 'would have been dead within five seconds.[76]'"

Scene 3—Neagle told reporters it was his responsibility to protect Judge Field adding, "I would have looked nice escorting a dead judge of the Supreme Court back to San Francisco.[77]'"

To other reporters who suggested that maybe he could have avoided lethal force to control Terry he replied, "If I'd got to close quarters with him, he could have bend me in two.... If I had hesitated, there would have been a different end to the affair. I'm sorry for the old man. But it was my duty and I had to do it[78]

Neagle later gave his version of the incident:

> "Justice Field and myself were at breakfast. I saw Terry coming. He approached Justice Field from behind. As he stood over him with clenched fists, as though about to strike him, or apparently to fall upon him in the excitement and anger, I sprang up and forward, and with my right hand grasped him by the coat, while I drew my revolver with my left. As he turned toward me I had him just right. I thrust the revolver forward and pulled twice. It was a self-actor and he fell[79]."

Scene 4 — A reporter for the *San Francisco Examiner*, paid a visit to Bertha while David was in jail:

> "Bertha staunchly defended her husband, saying she was confident he would be cleared of any wrongdoing, for she knew him to be

243

cool-headed and a man who never acts on the impulse of the moment and one who is a quick thinker and usually right. She denied that he was a gunfighter who had downed a man in Arizona and another in Montana, saying that she had been with him all the time and that there was absolutely no truth to the reports.[80]"

Scene 5—On April 14, 1890, the Supreme Court ruled in a 6-2 decision that Neagle "was acting under the authority of the law of the United States and was justified in so doing; and that he is not liable to answer in the courts of California on account of his part in that transaction." Defending judges is a duty of an officer of the court and does not require a specific statue.

This decision was codified in Cunningham v. Neagle U.S. 1;10S.Ct.658;34L.Ed.55 (1890).

Act V

After this final ruling, David and Bertha Neagle stayed in California for the rest of their lives. The oversized, misguided David Terry was dead. The dramatic lover, Sarah Althea Hill Sharon Terry, descended into insanity wandering the streets of San Francisco. She was eventually diagnosed with "dementia praecox," later known as schizophrenia. Judge Field continued on the bench for another ten years until his retirement.

The End of the Greek Tragedy!

Time To Take Off The Guns

After the Judge Field episode, David Neagle was in high demand as a bodyguard, which led him to security jobs guarding executives with the Southern Pacific Railroad, the United Railroad, and for Senator William Steward of Nevada.

However, in spite of his success in security employment, David still saw himself as a miner, and in 1912, when he was 65 years old, he did, in fact, hold a job as mine superintendent in Tuolumne County, California.

David and Bertha lived in San Francisco until about 1910, when they moved across the bay to Oakland. The 1910 census listed 62-year-old David Neagle as a "gold miner," and again in the 1920, census he listed his occupation as "mining," obviously his first love.

His daughter Winnie married August Halter and son Albert worked as an electrician with the Telephone Company and later as a motion picture operator.

David Neagle died at home on November 28, 1925, at 78 years of age. Bertha died two years later.

David Neagle had suffered the loss of his mother at a young age and had suffered the poverty and ostracization of the Irish while living in Boston. However, it appears that he had good support from his father, and he did not experience the trauma of witnessing starvation in Ireland or the terrible sea journey on a coffin ship, as had Moriarty and Leavy.

Therefore, in comparison to the other two gunfighters, David seemed to be better able to fit in with society, succeed in a marriage relationship, and pursue success in his occupations. Sometimes his methods were impetuous, to say the least, but David Neagle always got the job done – and he always thought he was operating on the side of the law, even though others disagreed.

He is a good example of a second-generation Irish immigrant pursuing the American dream with the confidence that can only be gained by believing totally in that dream. David Neagle was a man of numerous talents. He succeeded in designing and opening a successful saloon in Panamint; negotiating a lucrative lumber contract in Montana; running for political office in Tombstone; as well as maintaining an athletic body and honing his skills as a marksman.

He also certainly saw himself as a man of great character, even though others would, at times, disagree with this assessment. It is as if whenever confronted with a criminal act, a Don Quixote complex would take over, and David would see himself as the one-and-only answer to protecting the public. He would take off on a great steed to rid the world of this perceived evil, almost to his own undoing.

And, even after coming close to being in serious trouble after one of these episodes, he would repeat the full scenario in a heartbeat, if needed.

Finally, in the last great finale of his public life he was once again able to act within a split second and save the life of honorable Judge Field. He finished his career in a noble act of great character, fulfilling his best self-image in full Don Quixote fashion. I do not think it ever got better than this for any gunfighter in the old West.

[65] "I seldom advise parties": Schafer, op. cit

[66] "Perfect hive of human beings": History of Irish Americans in Boston - Wikipedia

[67] "During the present Decade": Governor Gardner, Massachusetts 1855 speech. Sec. State, ma.us/Irish immigration and know Nothings.

[68] "He pitched a tent": De Arment, op. cit

[69] "David Nagel(sic) a good prospector": De Arment, op. cit

[70] "Nagel(sic) was very much": De Arment, op. cit.

[71] "Square man who could not": De Arment, op. cit.

[72] "He was a fast gun": De Arment, op.cit

[73] "His hasty ungovernable temper": De Arment, op. cit

[74] "When he was finally": De Arment, op. cit.

[75] "Stop that, I am a United States Marshall": De Arment, op. cit.

[76] "Justice Field testified": De Arment, op. cit

[77] "I would have looked nice": De Arment, op. cit

[78] "If I'd got to close quarters": De Arment, op. cit

[79] "Justice Field and myself": The Killing of Terry, San Francisco, Call.80(66): 16 Aug 5, 1896

[80] "Bertha staunchly defended": De Arment, op. cit

Part V Who Else Lived in Pioche?

Other Noted Boot Hill Denizens

While growing up in Pioche, my favorite "let's go exploring" pal was RaNae Morris. We met in third grade when her family moved to Pioche from the Prince mine near Castleton, as her father had taken a job as "the" lineman for the Lincoln County Power Company. The last lineman had been electrocuted on the job!

After High School, I had enrolled in college at UNR; RaNae chose BYU, and we both majored in English. In 2019, I approached RaNae about jointly writing some of the well-known "Pioche Main Street" stories, and compiling a book that the Pioche Chamber of Commerce could use in their marketing.

RaNae accepted the challenge, and we self-published "Boot Hill Stories." The stories are priceless, and this book would not be complete without a few additional stories about the unarmed characters wandering up and down Main Street.

Thank you, RaNae, for allowing me to include your stories. They add immeasurably to the richness of this book.

Fanny Peterson — Courtesan

The life and death of Fanny Peterson is a classic story of prostitutes in the American West. In lawless, isolated mining towns, homesick miners pined for women. Many single women of the time had no economic options. They came west and entered prostitution as a business decision, a decision with harsh results. Few made enough money to retire; and their lives were often ended by suicide, drug overdose, illness, or murder. Venereal disease was common.

Fanny Peterson referred to herself as "a Spanish courtesan," maybe to earn more for her services. Brothels on the frontier charged more for Caucasian – up-stairs girls than for Chinese, Black, or American Indian girls. "Spanish" does not appear on any of the brothel menus in the four brothel museums of the American West; but it may have seemed exotic and economically beneficial to Fanny. There is, however, another explanation. The Library of Congress has a late 1800's Mexican newspaper containing an advertisement for a cigar and tobacco factory. The three Mexican girls sketched in the advertisement are called "Spanish Beauties." Fanny Peterson may have been Mexican or even Panamanian.

Fanny Peterson was murdered by a man who had been her lover, Lyman Perry Fuller. According to the *Daily Alta California* newspaper, Fanny and Lyman were known to have violent quarrels. They were not living together. A year before her death, Lyman tried to burn her possessions and made several attempts on her life. On the morning of July 12, 1872, Lyman saw Fanny on the street as he was leaving home. He fired three shots at her. His first bullet shattered her right arm. Fanny collapsed in the street. Lyman fired the next two bullets as he stood over her. The second bullet missed her. The third went through her hip into her stomach. Lyman seems to have momentarily considered suicide as he put his pistol in his mouth. Then he pointed it toward the ground and fired.

Fanny Peterson died later that day after accusing Lyman of setting the Pearl Saloon on fire five weeks earlier and poisoning the hogs of a local farmer. She was the 80th burial in the Pioche Cemetery.

Lyman P. Fuller was arrested and sentenced to fifteen years in the penitentiary at Carson City. He was pardoned after eleven years, light punishment for the ruthless murder of Panama Jack, as Fanny was known in Pioche.

Frenchy Danis — Pioche Resident

Some of the bodies buried in Pioche Boot Hill Cemetery arrived there with knife wounds.

All the components needed for a fight to turn deadly were at Schultzbacker's Dance House on Meadow Valley Street on the evening of November 5, 1873. There was a drunk man who slapped an innocent bystander and then was stabbed by a man with a knife.

Edward "Frenchy" Danis entered the dance house shortly after midnight. He had been drinking and near the entrance, he slapped the face of a man named Mucahy. Mucahy had a defender, Robert McCullough, who said, "This is a quiet and inoffensive man." McCullough pulled a pocketknife and said that Frenchy was drunk. Words were exchanged; Frenchy told McCullough he could have a fight. Frenchy left the dance house after slapping his hand on the bar and saying he cared for no one.

Frenchy returned to Schultzbacker's where McCullough was standing by the bar holding his open pocketknife. McCullough suggested, "Come, let's have another dance."

Frenchy said, "Well I don't give a God damn for you."

McCullough answered. "Well, I don't suppose you do Frenchy."

255

Frenchy's final words were, "McCullough, I've got but one hand (his left hand was bandaged) but it's a God damn good one.[81]"

Frenchy punched first. McCullough punched back holding his open knife. He hit Frenchy in the throat and blood streamed out. McCullough turned and handed his knife to William Soule. McCullough ran out the front door of the dance house, back in the front door, and out the back door. He was pursued by Ben Hyde and James Davis. Hyde caught him in a drug store. He was arrested by Officer Kelly.

Kelly asked McCullough why he had cut Frenchy. McCullough answered, "I didn't cut him."

Then Kelly asked, "What did you run for?"

"I didn't run," was the reply.

"I guess," said Kelly, "You're mistaken, for I ran after you.[82]"

McCullough was arrested and taken to jail.

Frenchy died. McCullough was released on bail. He returned to work. In early 1874, still out on bail for knifing Frenchy, Robert McCullough's eyes were seriously damaged by an explosion in the Raymond and Ely's main shaft. He left Pioche seeking medical help and never returned.

From March 1868 through December 1875, more than forty people were shot with guns and buried in the Pioche Cemetery. In the same period, only five men were stabbed and buried. One was the 26-year-old Canadian, Edward "Frenchy" Danis, No. 207

burial in the Pioche cemetery. Stabbings were less common than shootings, but the results could be just as deadly.

Minnie Summers — Actor

Minnie Summers, who stage name was Mary E. Chapman, was a twenty-five-year-old actress from Philadelphia. In 1871, after a brief stay in California, she moved to Pioche. On October 26, 1873, she attempted suicide by drinking an ounce of laudanum.

At the time, laudanum was called "tincture of opium" as it contained 10% powdered opium. It was a working-class drug, largely taken by women. Men abused alcohol. Although the alcohol content was about 48%, laudanum was cheaper than a bottle of gin or whiskey because it was considered a medication and not taxed as alcohol. It had been commonly used since the 16th century to treat pain and coughs. It was not used by physicians to stop breathing; but that is what an overdose of laudanum does.

It is not known whether Minnie Summers was a laudanum addict when she came to Pioche, or whether she bought her first bottle of laudanum in Pioche because she knew it was an effective way to commit suicide. In 1873, laudanum was sold without a prescription; it would not require a prescription until 1914. Miss Summers could have purchased her bottle of laudanum in Pioche or any town or city from any doctor or pharmacy, simply by asking for it.

Initially, Miss summers was lucky. She was treated at the Pioche hospital and regained consciousness. She said she wanted to live. Recovery seemed possible;

but thirty-eight hours after she drank the laudanum, Minnie summers died on October 28, 1873.

The report of her death in the *Pioche Daily Record* makes it clear that Minnie summers had been working as a prostitute during her time in Pioche. The newspaper called her death,

".... the self-wrought death of a poor girl whose ways had ceased to be the ways of virtue and pleasantness and the rash importunity of whose desperation and remorsefulness had brought her to a sudden impulse to take a leap into death's mystery.[83]"

Her graveside services, conducted by Rev. Henry L. Badger, were "attended by a large number of women of her own class and carriages." Minnie Summers was burial No. 205 in the cemetery.

S.D. Potter — Saloon Owner

Surely, S.D. Potter is the only person buried in the Pioche cemetery to have been killed by a bullet passing through a stove. S.D. was the proprietor of Potter's Saloon on Meadow Valley Street, not the best saloon in Pioche.

S.D. Potter died in his saloon on the evening of May 8, 1873. The *Pioche Daily Record,* reported, "Last night, about eleven o'clock, S.D. Potter...was shot and instantly killed by a negro named Howard. Howard and two other colored men were playing cards in the saloon. Some say Potter himself being engaged in the game with them."

An argument began and Potter ordered Jefferson Howard to leave. Howard refused. Potter is reported to have said, "You damn son of a bitch, if you don't leave here, I'll put a hole through you." Howard was unarmed. Potter told him to go heel (arm) himself.

The *Pioche Daily Record* continued, "A few moments afterward Howard appeared at the door, hailing Potter with 'Look out there now. I'm going to turn loose.'" The shooting began. Howard was standing at the door. Potter was at the back of the saloon, behind a large box-stove. They were about 20 feet apart. The fifth or sixth bullet fired by Howard passed through the stove, striking Potter in the heart. Potter was killed instantly, and Howard took flight. He was chased by the customers in the saloon. Although a lynching was threatened, Howard was

arrested in a house on Cedar Street by two deputy
sheriffs and taken to jail.

Alcohol, late hours, and combustible tempers caused
many of the burials in Pioche's Boot Hill cemetery. S.
D. Potter was burial No. 165.

In 1870, three years before Jefferson Howard shot
S.D. Potter, four adult African American men lived in
Lincoln County. Only one of them, a porter named
H. Johnson, lived in Pioche. Jefferson Howard was
not one of the four.

Western American mining camps were ethnically
diverse; but the economic class structure was rigid.
White men owned and ran all the mines. Poor white
men, Mexicans, and Chinese were the miners,
working in the shafts. A few African American men,
who left the southern states after the Civil War,
worked in the mines; but most worked in service jobs.
Jefferson Howard, who had been a Union soldier,
came to Pioche after the summer of 1870, likely
dreaming of earning his fortune in a rich mining town
or at least getting steady work. Instead, he was found
guilty of manslaughter and received ten years hard
labor in the state penitentiary. He was pardoned after
about half of his sentence. In 1880 he was arrested in
Lyon County (Nevada) when, during an argument
about a horse race, he pulled his gun on a state
assemblyman.

Pierpont Thayer — Actor

The grand opening of Brown's Theatre in Pioche, which later became Tompson's Opera House, was held on September 16, 1873. Bella Bird's Players, an acting company from San Francisco leased the theatre for the opening. Miss Sallie Hinckley and Mr. Pierpont Thayer were the principal attractions. Their performance in the comedy "Pygmalion and Galatea" was a great success.

Pierpont Thayer had a good career, appearing in California and Nevada. In 1867, he was a 30-year-old actor living in San Francisco at Broadway and Montgomery streets. In February 1873, he played at the Carson Theatre and Piper's Opera House in Virginia City. Mr. Thayer and Miss Hinckley arrived in Pioche on September 10th on the Hamilton stagecoach.

It had been expected that on the evening of September 17th, the day after the grand opening, Mr. Thayer would be a featured player in "The Fortunes of a Poor Young Man;" but his part was played by a substitute actor.

Late in the evening of September 18, 1873, moans were heard coming from Mr. Thayer's room at Mrs. Caldwell's lodging house on Meadow Valley Street. His door was locked, and access was finally gained through his window. The men who entered the room found Pierpont Thayer lying on the floor undressed except for an undershirt. White frothy foam covered his mouth. An empty bottle of laudanum (opium) was on a table.

Mr. Thayer had been drinking for two days and was in the habit of taking laudanum when he drank. The laudanum bottle held just one ounce; but laudanum and alcohol were often a deadly combination. Some reports state he had lost his position with the acting company. He left a note written on sheet music. The words were, "I test the problem. Pierpont Thayer."

Two days after the grand opening of Brown's Theatre, Pierpont Thayer was dead and would be burial No. 196 in the Pioche cemetery.

In 1908, Gelett Burges (1866-1951) wrote "The Heart Line," a book about the spiritualists, fortune tellers, and outright con artists who worked in San Francisco before the 1906 earthquake and fundamentally changed the city. In Chapter VII of "The Heart Line," there is a discussion about Pierpont Thayer:

"I was just a-thinkin 'about Pierpont Thayer. Don't You remember that dope who went nuts on spiritualism and committed suicide?"

"No, I don't recall it, what about it?"

"He got all wound up in the circles here – Sadie Crum, she had him on the string for a year, till he didn't know where he was at. He took it so hard that one day he up and shot hisself and left a note pinned on to the bed that said, 'I go to test the problem.'"

"I would have sold every one of my tricks and all of hers to Him for a five-dollar bill! Why didn't he come to me to test his problem?"

......" Them that want to believe are goin' to, and you can't prevent 'em no matter what you do. They're like hop fiends – they've got to have their dope whether or no, and just so long as they can dream it out they're happy.[84]"

Pierpont Thayer did not shoot himself. But Gelett Burgess added an intriguing third possible cause for Thayer's suicide: alcohol, laudanum, and, perhaps, spiritualism.

Boot Hill

"Not every western American town had a public cemetery nicknamed "Boot Hill." The first Boot Hill cemeteries were in the cattle towns of Hays and Dodge City, Kansas. Many of the cemetery occupants were cowboys who 'died with their boots on' in gunfights, beatings, stabbings, and hangings. There are other famous boot Hills in Tombstone, Arizona and deadwood, South Dakota."

"Boot Hill cemeteries began as public cemeteries, The first victim likely arrived at the cemetery with a fatal gunshot wound. But it wasn't long before gunfighters, claim jumpers, and cowboys were buried next to housewives, farmers, judges, miners, and children[85]."

"The Pioche Boot Hill cemetery is not unique. It is, instead, an absolutely classic example of a Boot Hill of the American west. It began, and continues to be, the local public cemetery. Between 1868 and 1875, 269 people were buried here. For the most part, the gunfighters are buried next to the gamblers. People who came to Pioche for the silver strike may have thought they would eventually be going down the road to the next mining discovery. "

However, hundreds of them are buried in Pioche and could not make that choice. The silence, the smell of sagebrush, and the sounds of the historic tram add to the solemnity of the cemetery. Real people with dreams and aspirations were buried here."

"In Pioche, the terms 'Boot Hill' and 'cemetery' both refer to the Pioche public cemetery. The cemetery must have been established in March 1868, when saloonkeeper, Frank Pitt, was fatally shot by Jacob Colburn. Mr. Pitt was the first person buried in the public cemetery. By 1873, the public cemetery had more than a hundred graves. Women and children were buried there, but most of the graves were for adult males.

Many graves were for victims of mining accidents; but during that period, 30 men died as victims of homicide. The public cemetery did have a loosely defined segregated area called 'Murder's Row.' Although exact burial places are not recorded in the 1800's, it can be assumed that Murder's Row was reserved for gunslingers, claim jumpers, and of course murderers. Because many of the men buried in the cemetery died with their boots on, sometime in the past the cemetery was given the 'Boot Hill' nickname."

The Pioche Daily Record described the cemetery in 1873: There were "Rude headstones with inscriptions written in pencil." Many graves had "nothing to indicate the name or nativity of the dead." Approximately 25 graves had actual headstones. One hand-carved wood grave marker recorded, "Shot by a coward while working his claim no one even knew his name. Pioche Nev." *The Record* also complained, "The public cemetery ought to be enclosed, for it is no credit to our camp that its dead should be interred in an open field.'"

It is not true that 72 people died in gunfights and were buried in the cemetery before anyone died of natural causes. The reality is interesting and more diverse. The first 72 burials include four people who were believed to be poisoned by unclean water, one pneumonia victim, a possible cholera victim, and eleven men who died in the horrific fire of September 1871.

The Pioche public cemetery, also known as 'Boot Hill'; is movingly evocative of the mining camps of the American frontier. The cemetery is directly underneath an aerial tramway, original to the mining operations of the 1920's and 1930's. The buckets sway in the wind on thick cables. Almost a hundred years ago, those buckets carried silver and nickel ore from the mines to the Godbe Mill. If you visit the cemetery, you might hear, above the silence, the sound of mine bells, the noisy machinery of the mills, and laughter coming from saloons.

---

[81] "Come let's have another dance": Schafer, op. cit
[82] "What did you run for?": Pioche Daily Record, November 6, 1873
[83] "The self-wrought death of a poor girl": Schafer op. cit
[84] "I was just thinkin'": Gelett Burges, "The Heart Line", 1908, Create Space (May 27, 2015)
[85] "Not every western": Making Spaces on the Western Frontier, Paul Reeve, University of Illinois Press, 2008

Epilogue

During the two-year period of researching and writing this book, I pondered the idea of traveling to Ireland in order to gain further understanding of the three Irish gunfighters about whom I had chosen to write. Would it help the book, I wondered? Would I uncover more information from the mid-1800's about these men? Would it deepen my understanding of their culture?

By Spring of 2023, I became convinced that I should make the investment in a trip to Cahersiveen, Ireland, the birthplace of Richard Moriarty, fully realizing that it was impossible to know what I would gain from the experience. At some point, you either take the chance or you don't — it's a roll of the dice; and, after all, I'm part Irish and live in Nevada, a gambling State!

My husband and I landed at Dublin airport April 22, 2023, about 3:00 p.m. tired, but very excited and pumped up. It was gray skies and chilly, and it stayed gray skies and chilly for the next two weeks. My advice is to never go to Ireland without three layers of clothing, and don't expect the inside of the buildings to be warmer than the outside — it won't happen! This is what stout beer and Jameson's whiskey are for.

We had briefly wondered about transportation to Cahersiveen, but I was sure that it was no problem. After all, there are trains and buses all over Ireland. After a few days sightseeing, we arrived in Killarney, our southwest Ireland travel hub. It's a cute tourist town close to the west coast, and a place where Dubliners like to go for the weekend. It's close to Cahersiveen and the beautiful Ring of Kerry, located on the Iveragh Peninsula.

However, we soon discovered there is no train operating on this peninsula; and other than tour buses, there is one bus going in each day and one bus returning, and the times of arrival and departure are only two hours apart. It became apparent that we had to rent a car and drive the 50 miles on the left side of a narrow, winding road to Cahersiveen, because I had an 11:00 A.M appointment with the head librarian at the Cahersiveen Library, Noreen O'Sullivan.

We made the drive without incident, and then the real fun began. Noreen is a soft spoken, educated, attractive, efficient librarian with quite a bit of experience in genealogy. We both loved our subject, the illusive, Richard Moriarty, born in Noreen's hometown. We connected immediately and couldn't talk fast enough.

Noreen explained the problems of Irish genealogical research and gave me needed guidance on whether I could ever expect to find any more information about Richard over and above what I had. The upshot is that it would be difficult, very time-consuming, and could still be fruitless. This is because Cahersiveen, a small town, was, in the 1800's, surrounded by small villages consisting of mostly under 10 families called Townlands. People in the Townlands would most often refer to the larger town when stating where they live. Therefore, Richard and his family were probably residents of a small Townland and there are many, most of which had their own Catholic church and baptism records. This would result in an exhaustive search.

At that point, I told Noreen that I would like to meet some interested people in Cahersiveen, and hopefully, some Moriarty descendants. I offered to give a small talk about the Moriarty gunfighter in a local restaurant or pub, since the library needed permission from the main location in Tralee, which would take weeks. Noreen suggested the "Shabeen" pub next door to the library, and that I should go talk to Phil O'Sullivan, the owner.

Curious about the name of the pub, I googled "Shabeen" and found that it means a location for the sale of illegal alcohol liquor. In other words, it's a "speakeasy," however, Phil is now selling legal liquor. What fun!

The "Shabeen" is in an old building, probably of 1800's vintage. The bar probably has room for eight to ten stools and several tables with benches and a few chairs. Four Irish men were holding up the bar mid-afternoon, mid-week. The walls are covered with newspaper clippings, posters, affirmations, pictures, etc. all placed randomly at different times. The "Shabeen" has a back room with six or seven tables, chairs, and a faux fireplace in one corner for special events.

My new friend, Phil, agreed to allow me to use the backroom the next day at 5:00 p.m., if I could, in fact, draw some people to the talk. I promised to give it a try.

At that point, I decided that my only hope of making this happen was to go door to door to all the businesses in Cahersiveen, a three-block town on the Ring of Kerry. I started down one side of the street and up the other—barbershop, dress shop, fish monger, newspaper/grocery, health food, hairdresser, plus coffee shop where I interrupted four women socializing. This group was really interested (I lucked out) and said they would call Moriarty friends and would, for sure, attend.

It looked like I might draw 10 to 15 folks, so I hurried back to the "Shabeen" and sealed the deal for 5:00 the next day. I was then introduced to one of the four men at the bar as a "Moriarty." He was friendly; and, I think, was telling me his full genealogical heritage; but his brogue, thick as molasses, along with probably a couple of pints of stout that afternoon prohibited further conversation — my loss!

So back to Killarney on the left side of the teeny, tiny road for the night, and to plan my talk. "Here goes nothing," I said to myself, but at least I could go home knowing that I had tried my best. The next day we took off for the 50 miles to Cahersiveen once again, now feeling more confident on the road and enjoying the rich green rolling hills and valleys. Of course, Ireland is truly as beautiful as is advertised and the people are without a doubt friendly and very accommodating. They do go out of their way to be helpful to strangers.

At 3:00 p.m. I started revisiting the" Shabeen" along with the local businesses to let everyone know I was in town and ready to talk. At 4:30 Darryl and I were in the bar — Darryl enjoying a pint of stout and me with my diet Pepsi and a stomach full of butterflies!

At 5:00 no one was there, and I was about ready to order a Jameson, when five women, who had entered through the back door, surrounded me, and exclaimed, "Are you the writer?"

Wow! We moved to the back room where Phil had arranged the table and chairs and had turned on the faux fireplace. The ladies all introduced themselves. Two were sisters, Mary and Ann Moriarty, two were their neighbors, and Noreen, the librarian, had joined us, as well. Everyone was ready to talk about Richard Moriarty, the gunfighter from their hometown.

Mary asked if I had a photograph. There are no photographs, but I do have a copy of a courthouse drawing, which I had brought with me. Mary said, "Look, Ann, at this drawing; we have a bunch of relatives who look just like this!"

As I told Richard's history from his birth during the famine, to his emigrating to Australia, New Zealand, British Columbia, Idaho, and finally Nevada, the ladies were quickly bonding with their long, lost clansman. I know for sure that this was happening because I carefully explained that Richard had been involved in some killings during the gunfighting and that they might be shocked. I told them of the killing of O'Toole in the bar in Virginia City. All five of the ladies laughed, and one exclaimed, "oh, the lad shot another Irishman, did he," followed by group laughter.

Noreen had said earlier when I tried to gently warn her of Richard's violent tendencies, "But, we don't know what the lad had been through. There but for the grace of God go I." The "lad" won over the ladies that day, and he has been dead for 150 years. Oh, the luck of the Irish!

I have an offer for book sales at the "Quirke's Newsagent's" store at 2 Main Street, Cahersiveen, and I plan to return for a book signing. In fact, I can't wait to visit my new friends there.

I left Cahersiveen that evening with my feet "not" touching the ground. It was an almost "out of body" experience of a lifetime. Now we were back on the train to Dublin.

The next day's plan was for a tour of the "Jeanie Johnston" — an exact replica of a famous Irish famine ship. Most English-owned famine ships lost a large percentage of their passengers to death caused by infectious diseases. The "Jeanie Johnston" made 16 Atlantic crossings and did not lose one life. Their success was due to rigid sanitation rules, exact amounts of selected food for each passenger, and a physician on board for every crossing.

There were about 15 of us on the tour that day. When we got ready to descend into the hull of the ship, we all took a deep breath, as we knew this would be an up close and personal experience. The 15 of us fit comfortably in the hull and were enjoying looking around at the inside of the ship, until we saw the "human dummies" lined up three abreast in the wooden sleeping cribs divided into three levels.

There was an immediate silence, and then the guide explained that the crossings were made with 180 to 200 passengers living in the area where the 15 of us were standing. The silence in the hull turned into a collective gasp!

We tried to lighten up the next few days with tours of the National Art Museum, Trinity College and shopping for woolen gifts; but we both knew that we would forever be changed by our experiences in Ireland, the land of great stout beer, whiskey, unimaginable natural beauty, but laced with a bitter past.

Ode To A Shootist

Shooting stars,

Across the sky.

Continents passing,

As you fly.

Long coat flying,

High above.

Don't stop now,

Beware of love.

You fly so high,

Your gun is burning.

Whirl a Hurdie,

Ignore the yearning.

Two cards up,

Ace is high.

Flying faster,

Who will die?

No judgement here,

Advice is naught.

For shooting stars,

Take first shot!

Acknowledgements

My deepest thanks to my husband, Darryl Martin, who magically thinks most of my ideas are worth listening to, and who fully supports everything that I write. Thanks to my readers, Linda Faiss Amstutz, Patty Jacobsen, and to Kathy Hilty who valiantly took a deep dive into a multitude of revisions to bring this book to the finish line. Also, Nicola Collins, a native Dubliner, guided me through my research into Irish history, the famine era, and facilitated calls to contacts in Cahersiveen. Finally, this book would not have been complete without the additional stories written by RaNae Travers and by the background we shared together as childhood friends.

Eneclann of Dublin and genealogist, Judith Edmonds of Australia, were most helpful in their research regarding the heritage and travel of Richard Moriaty. It was a tough "ask."

The Pioche authors who took the first initiative to record the full history of Pioche, James Hulse and Leo Schafer, along with Corrine Fullerton Shumway and Peggy Draper Hone, authors of "I Dig Pioche", are due enormous credit for their heavy lifting. Also, a huge thanks to Amanda Choquer of the Lincoln County Clerk's office who dug deep into the basement of the Lincoln County Courthouse to find the *"State of Nevada v Morgan Courtney"* trial. The discovery of this trial was key to making this book possible.

Several other Nevada journalists have given me encouragement and support to continue with my Nevada history research: Authors John L. Smith, Sally Denton, Michael Green, Curtis Vickers, editor of the University of Nevada Press, as well as the late Margaret Dalrymple. In closing, I wish to acknowledge the educational system of the State of Nevada for providing me with the tools to write this book.